DECISION MAKING AT CHILD WELFARE INTAKE

A Handbook for Practitioners

DECISION MAKING AT CHILD WELFARE INTAKE

A Handbook for Practitioners

Theodore J. Stein
and
Tina L. Rzepnicki

Jane Addams College of Social Work
University of Illinois
Chicago, Illinois

CHILD WELFARE LEAGUE OF AMERICA, INC.
67 Irving Place, New York, New York

Child Welfare League of America
67 Irving Place, New York, NY 10003

Copyright © 1983 by the Child Welfare League of America, Inc.

Current printing (last digit)
10 9 8 7 6 5 4 3 2 1

Printed in the United States of America

Library of Congress Cataloging in Publication Data

Stein, Theodore J.
    Decision making at child welfare intake.

    Includes bibliographical references.
    1. Child welfare—United States.   2. Foster home
care—United States.   I. Rzepnicki, Tina L.   II. Title.
HV741.S744   1983   362.7′1   83-2030
ISBN 0-87868-213-9

ACKNOWLEDGMENT

This research was supported by a grant from the United States Children's Bureau, U.S. Department of Health and Human Services, grant number 90-CW-2043 (02).

ACKNOWLEDGMENT

This research was supported in part by a grant from the United States Children's Bureau, U.S. Department of Health and Human Services.

AUTHORS

Theodore J. Stein received his D.S.W. from the University of California at Berkeley. He is Associate Professor at the Jane Addams College of Social Work, University of Illinois at Chicago. Dr. Stein was director of the Alameda Project, an experimental effort to counter "foster care drift." His publications in child welfare include *Children in Foster Homes: Achieving Continuity-in-Care* and *Social Work Practice in Child Welfare*, plus numerous articles and chapters in anthologies.

Tina L. Rzepnicki is Research Associate and Lecturer at the Jane Addams College of Social Work, University of Illinois at Chicago, where she teaches practice methods to graduate students. Dr. Rzepnicki received her Ph.D. from the School of Social Service Administration, The University of Chicago. She has been heavily involved in projects devoted to technical assistance to public child welfare agencies, parent education, child welfare curriculum development, and intake decision making.

CONTENTS

                                                                    Page

INTRODUCTION 1

  A Model for Decision Making 2
     Key Processes 3
     Information 5
  Worker Judgment as a Decision-Making Variable 7
  Limitations 8
  Organization of the Manual 9
  References 11

Chapter One   PHASE I—RECEPTION 13

  Protective Services and Voluntary Services—
    Differences at Reception 14
  Protective Services 14
     Using Information for Decision Making 16
     Criteria for an Immediate Home Visit 18
  Voluntary Child Welfare Services 19
     Determining the General Nature of the Presenting Problem
      and the Circumstances Surrounding Onset 21
     Is Assistance Needed with Assessment or Investigative
      Tasks? 25
  For Discussion 26
  References 28

Page

**Chapter Two   PHASE II—INVESTIGATION AND PROBLEM
ASSESSMENT** 29

The Investigation 30
Guidelines for Determining Whether a Child Is in Immediate
    Danger and Whether Protective Custody Is Necessary 34
Determining Whether There is Credible Evidence of Abuse or
    Neglect 45
    Types of Evidence 48
    A Note on Gathering and Recording Information 50
    Using Information to Determine Whether There Is
        Credible Evidence of Abuse or Neglect 50
    Examples 52
    A Note on Risk Taking 55
Is It Necessary to Petition the Court? 58
Is Out-of-Home Placement Necessary? 59
What Is the Most Appropriate Placement Facility? 61
Problem Assessment 62
    The Purpose of Assessment: An Overview 63
Beginning Assessment 65
    Information from Records and Service Providers 65
    Protective Service Problem Profile 67
Interviewing All Family Members: A Framework for
    Gathering Initial Assessment Information 67
    Family Interaction 72
Evaluating Assessment Strategies 73
    Client Self-Reports 73
    Direct Observation by Professionals 75
    Collateral Resources 76
    Information in Case Records, Court Reports, and Central
        Registries 76
Identifying Assessment Strategies 77
    Problem Selection 77
General Guidelines for Selecting Assessment Strategies 78
Formulating and Using Hypotheses to Guide Selection of
    Assessment Strategies 79
    The Richards Family 79
    Issues in Assessment 82
    The Innes Family 86
Criteria for Deciding Whether to Open a Case for Voluntary
    Services 90
For Discussion 94
References 101

Page

Chapter Three   PHASE III—SERVICE PLANNING 103

The Contents of Written Service Agreements 104
    Case Goals 104
    Problem-Solving Objectives 107
    Tasks 110
    Time Limits 112
    Consequences 112
    Multiple Uses of Service Agreements 112
Selecting Problem-Solving Strategies 113
    A Note on the Selection of Counseling Programs 117
Guidelines for Selecting Service Strategies 118
Written Service Agreements 120
    Service Agreement—The Richards Family 120
    Amending Service Agreements 122
    Service Agreement—The Innes Family 123
Monitoring Client Progress in Service Delivery Programs 128
For Discussion 129
References 130

FIGURES

		Page
0.1	Decision-Making Model (Diagram)	3
1.1	Is an Immediate Home Visit Necessary? (Flow Chart)	15
1.2	Voluntary Service Reception—Close or Refer for Assessment? (Flow Chart)	20
1.3	Problem Profile (Form With Voluntary Service Example)	22
1.4	Client Contact Log (Form With Case Example)	24
1.5	Is Assistance Required: Assessment/Investigation? (Flow Chart)	25
2.1	Is Child in Danger? Can Child Be Safeguarded at Home or Is Protective Custody Necessary? (Flow Chart)	33
2.2	Checklist: Observations From First Home Visit (Checklist)	42
2.3	Sources of Information for Determining Whether There Is Credible Evidence of Abuse or Neglect (List)	46
2.4	Is There Credible Evidence of Abuse or Neglect? (Flow Chart)	49
2.5	Is There Credible Evidence That Abuse or Neglect Had Occurred or That the Child Is at Risk of Either? (Form)	56
2.6	Is It Necessary to Petition the Court? (Flow Chart)	58
2.7	Is Out-of-Home Placement Necessary? (Flow Chart)	60
2.8	What Is the Most Appropriate Placement Facility? (Flow Chart)	61
2.9	What Are the Specific Problems in Need of Resolution? (Flow Chart)	66
2.10	Information Regarding Use of Services (Form)	68
2.11	Problem Profile (Form With Protective Services Example)	70
2.12	Client Interview Memo (Form With Case Example)	73

                                                                        Page
2.13   Form for Recording Moods and Related Activities
       (Form With Case Example) 89
2.14   Form for Recording Arguments and Related Issues
       (Form With Case Example) 89
2.15   Form to Record Returning From School and Chore Completion
       (Form With Case Example) 91
2.16   Problem Profile—Richards Family (Form With Case
       Example) 98
2.17   Problem Profile—Innes Family (Form With Case Example).....100
3.1   The Case Planning Process (Flow Chart) 105
3.2   Service Agreement With the Richards Family
       (Case Example) 120
3.3   Amendment to Service Agreement With the Richards Family
       (Case Example) 123
3.4   Plan for Negotiation Training (Case Example) 124
3.5   Service Agreement With the Innes Family (Case Example) 124
3.6   Plan to Maintain a Division of Responsibility for Household
       Chores (Case Example) 125
3.7   Plan to Increase the Frequency With Which Mr. Innes
       Engages in Activities That He Identifies as Positive
       (Case Example) 126
3.8   Plan to Establish a Men's Group (Case Example) 127

INTRODUCTION

THIS MANUAL DESCRIBES procedures for decision making at child welfare intake for both protective services and voluntary child welfare services. The methods reported here were developed under a grant from the United States Children's Bureau. They were field tested in regional offices of two public welfare agencies in two states and in one voluntary agency that provides protective services under contract to one of the state agencies.

Intake is a process that begins with a request for services or report of abuse or neglect and continues through development of a service plan. The decisions made at intake are some of the most important ones made by child welfare staff. This is the point at which clients are granted or denied agency services. In addition, what happens to families who receive services may be determined by the choices made at intake. For example, the use of weak decision-making strategies has resulted in children entering foster care without consideration of ways of maintaining them in their own homes, and has contributed to the drift of children in out-of-home placement [23:8–34].

For almost a decade, professional attention has focused on developing guidelines for decision making that would increase the likelihood that children in out-of-home placement would be reunited with their biological parents or placed in alternative settings where they would receive continuity in care [17;22]. Correctly so. Finding permanent homes for young people, many of whom experience multiple foster home placements during their tenure in the child welfare system, is of the utmost importance [19:117–118]. But permanency planning must begin at intake. All decisions made from the point of entry into the child welfare system must address the question, Will the choices selected further or impede progress toward the goal of permanency?

Since decision-making procedures for moving children out of placement are already available, it is time to back up and develop guidelines for intake decisions. Accomplishing this task will provide direction to workers for making all of the decisions from the point of entry into the system through case termination.

A MODEL FOR DECISION MAKING

Figure 0.1 presents a model to serve as a guide in developing procedures and rules for decision making [24]. The goals of any system provide a reference point against which the decision maker must weigh and balance options. Stated otherwise, each time a decision is made, the question, Which option is most likely to facilitate attainment of a system goal? must be asked.

The goals of the child welfare system reflect social values. The right of biological parents to raise their own children and the right of children to be raised by their family of origin is foremost. When evidence shows that parents cannot or will not raise their children, attention must shift to the child's right to be raised in an alternative setting that maximizes the youngster's chances for continuity in care.

Figure 0.1 **DECISION-MAKING MODEL**

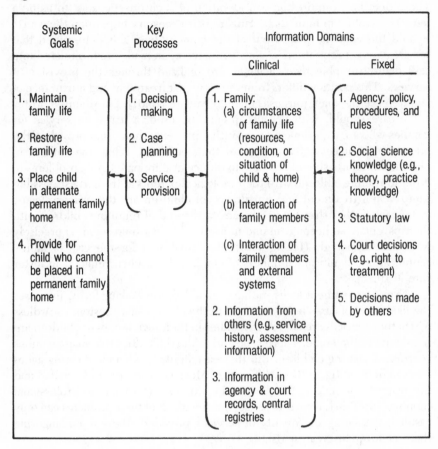

The goals shown in figure 0.1 represent a preferred hierarchy for achieving permanency by (1) maintaining family life through the provision of services in the child's own home; (2) reuniting with their biological families children who are in foster care; (3) placing in permanent homes through adoption or court appointment of a legal guardian children who cannot remain with or be returned to their own families; and (4) arranging planned long-term placements for youngsters who cannot or should not be placed in legally binding relationships.

Key Processes

Decision making is the key to achieving the system's goals. For each case, a series of decisions must be made that result in either the development of a case plan or the determination that the family will not receive services. These decisions require the consideration of such questions as (to name a few): Is the child in immediate danger? Is it necessary to petition the court? Should the child be placed out of the home? Once it is determined that services are appropriate, decisions that have been made are formulated into case plans, the objectives of which are realized through the provision of services. This position differs from the view that treatment and nurturance of children are the main purposes of child welfare [28:61]. For example, foster home care should, with few exceptions, be used as a respite service for families who are experiencing a crisis that prevents them from providing the minimal care necessary to safeguard their children. While the child is in placement, efforts should be made to reduce or eliminate family problems in order to reunite children with their biological parents at the earliest possible time. When treatment and nurturance of children are the primary focus, foster care, rather than being a means to the end of reuniting children with their parents, can become an end in itself. This, it would seem, is precisely what has happened. Having substituted treatment for the goal of family reunification, significant numbers of children have been retained in foster care [6;19;23].

Use of a treatment focus, rather than a decision-making focus, increases the likelihood of cases being retained in the child welfare system regardless of whether services are offered to families in their own homes or children are placed out of the home. There is no end to the difficulties that many families confront in rearing children. But there are limits to what child caring agencies can do to mitigate these difficulties. Most agencies are understaffed and the majority of children are served by workers who have no professional training [19:77–81]. Efforts to assist clients with all of their problems can only result in lessening the quality of services provided, thereby endangering those children at greatest risk.

We are not suggesting that families be left with problems unresolved. Rather, child welfare agencies must be put into the context of a community's total service delivery system and distinctions made between the mission of child welfare programs and other community programs.

With regard to children in out-of-home care, limiting the range of problems is essential if we are to realize permanency goals within reasonable periods of time. We know that the likelihood of reuniting children with their biological parents is greatest during a child's first year to 18 months in care, and the likelihood of achieving adoption is greatest during the next 18-month period. Following 3 years in placement, the chances of leaving the foster care system in any way are markedly reduced [23:86–87,113]. Thus, workers must focus their attention on a narrow range of problems that must be remediated to ensure the safety of children. With this accomplished, families can be referred to others in the community for help with problems that do not bear directly on issues of a child's well-being.

Information

The data base for decision making must take into account both clinical and fixed information domains and the interaction between the two. Clinical information is relatively fluid. Workers must decide what areas of family life to assess; where, when, and how to conduct an assessment; and whom to interview outside of the nuclear family. Fixed information, agency policy, statutory law, court decisions, and social science knowledge, for example, change over time, but remain relatively constant during the early stages of a case when some of the most critical decisions affecting a child's future are made. Fixed information sets limits to a worker's autonomy in selecting options. Thus, a clinical decision may lead to the conclusion that a child is experiencing emotional neglect or abuse, but if a state's statutes do not include these conditions as a basis for protective service action, it may not be possible to provide services unless parents request them.

Social science theory and knowledge give direction to the process of gathering clinical information and of using this information for decision making. Identifying and respecting the limits of knowledge were areas of concern in undertaking to describe the data base for each decision. The troublesome issues are exemplified in the current debate over a correct standard for decision making [2:97–138; 8; 9; 11:55–61; 26:645–693].

Historically, child welfare workers have been admonished to make decisions in the best interests of the child. The values implied in the best interests standard, while laudable in intent, are an impediment to decision making. If values are to guide the decision maker they must reflect attainable rather than ideal ends, since they are the basis for articulation of decision-making criteria and rules. If values reflect ideals whose attainment is beyond current knowledge and available technology, procedures for realizing them cannot be described.

Once one moves beyond a child's minimum needs, there is neither professional nor social consensus as to what is in any child's best interests. Thus, the worker who is admonished to make decisions using the best interests of the child as a standard for evaluating parental adequacy is left with a vacuum. This vacuum is defined as the distance between minimum standards that we know or think necessary for maximizing child development in areas such as medical, emotional, educational, supervision, and shelter needs, and the ideals implied by this standard. Workers are caught in a bind. They are told to make decisions using a standard but are not given guidance as to what conditions would constitute the presence of the implied ideal. Child welfare staff, then, interject their personal biases and values into the decision-making process [3:167;6:43–44;15:84].

Also, the best interests standard requires the decision maker to predict the long-range effects on children of their relations with parents and significant others. The state of knowledge is not sufficient for making that prediction [8:6; 14:1117–1153; 20:354; 27:130].

If the decision maker focuses on minimum standards of parenting, with a requirement that intervention proceed only if there is evidence that children have been harmed or will be at risk in the near future, the best interests of children are more likely to be served where best interest is defined in relation to what is possible given the limits of knowledge at any time. Moreover, a focus on minimum standards reinforces the value that our society places on family privacy—on the right of parents to raise their children free of outside intervention—while simultaneously protecting a child's right to be safeguarded from undue harm as well as the right to be raised by the family of origin. The best interests standard leaves a wide margin for subjectivity and individual biases to influence decisions as to when intervention should occur, thereby undermining these values.

A focus on minimum standards facilitates describing the data base for decision making and the establishment of decision-making rules. For example, rather than being concerned with a parent's use of drugs or alcohol, one would ask the question, How is the child being harmed by such behaviors or what harm might be expected to occur if substance abuse continues? Assessment would focus on the child's needs for supervision, medical care, and other areas noted above. Consider the area of supervision. During assessment, the worker's attention would focus on issues such as the child's self-help skills (e.g., her* ability to dial an emergency telephone number, knowledge of how to cross the street, information that she has regarding whom to turn to in the event of an emergency), the parent's knowledge of the child's ability to care for herself and whether these are realistic in relation to the child's self-help skills, resources that are available to assist the youngster if the need for help should arise when the parent is not present (e.g., neighbors or relatives to whom the child can turn), and the availability and affordability of child care resources, such as day care. Information from any one of these areas would be viewed in relation to information from other areas, and the decision made to intervene or not.

The importance of identifying a minimum data base for each decision,

*For simplicity and consistency in this handbook, the child is referred to in the feminine, the worker in the masculine, and the parent or caretaker and the caller or reporter in the feminine. Parent is generally singular.

and of establishing rules for adding to this data base incrementally when the minimum information proves insufficient for decision making, cannot be overstated. Copious amounts of information are a hindrance to making decisions. And the evidence shows that workers gather data far in excess of what is actually needed for making decisions [4; 7:289–296; 12; 21:91,278; 29:72–73].

WORKER JUDGMENT AS A DECISION-MAKING VARIABLE

Readers of this manual may find that its approach to decision making restricts worker autonomy in exercising professional judgment to make decisions. This effort is deliberate. The reasoning is as follows.

The decisions made by child welfare staff members have a significant impact on the lives of their clients. If worker judgment is to serve as a basis for decisions that result in reducing family autonomy, limiting family privacy and, at times, separating parents and children, it must be justified by evidence that its application yields gains that outweigh the costs to the families being served. "Empirical evidence . . . indicates that professional judgment is too often inaccurate and inconsistent [for decision making]" [1:8].

Significant research effort has gone into uncovering the principles that guide child welfare staff members in making critical choices. Unfortunately, constant principles of practice have not been discerned [24]. The extent to which individual values and biases have been shown to influence decision making is very troublesome. It raises questions as to whether what we refer to as professional judgment would, when observed in lay people, be called simple bias.

The authors do not seek to eliminate the role of professional judgment, but rather are concerned with identifying ways of describing what is meant by this term, and of minimizing the likelihood that individual biases will influence work with clients. The paucity of prescriptive literature on clinical decision making has contributed to the difficulties workers confront. Social work literature is rich in outlining categories in which information should be elicited from and about clients but is rather impoverished in describing how this information is to be used [5;16].

Moreover, social work practice in child welfare has changed markedly in recent years. Whether one considers the increased formality of juvenile court procedures, the growth in litigation against child-caring agencies, the frequency with which each of the parties with a vested interest in the disposition of a case is represented by separate counsel, the substantive case-planning requirements found in federal and state legislation, or the growing acceptance of 18-month dispositional hearings for children in placement, the trend toward a more legal approach to practice is clear [10;13:18;25].

Workers can expect to have their decisions challenged by review boards or by attorneys representing children or their biological or foster parents, and to have to support their choices with factual evidence, not, as in the past, with impressions and judgments that are not supported by objective data.

LIMITATIONS

The authors are mindful of the many constraints under which child welfare workers operate. Resource deficits may prevent staff from carrying out the most carefully planned decision. If consultation from other professionals is not available, workers may not be able to create the data base needed for making choices. Inservice training in the use of decision-making procedures is necessary, and administration must provide incentives to staff for goal-oriented behavior.

Some but not all of these limitations can be addressed within a decision-making framework. It can be argued that services to families in their own home—day care and homemaker services, for example—should be used to prevent placement. But if services are not available, and there is reason to think that a child will be at risk of injury if left in the care of her parents without services, removal may be necessary. Guidelines for documenting existing risks, how the risks can be avoided with services, and how they may persist when services are not available, appear in this manual. Rigorous documentation allows workers to clarify the basis for their choices, including identification of preferred options and the supports and barriers in the system to implementing options. Likewise, staff members can document the constraints imposed on them when they do not have access to consultants. A worker who suspects that a child is suffering from emotional abuse, but whose training precludes a rigorous assessment of this issue, can document his suspicions, as such, and note that definitive conclusions cannot be reached.

Resolution to problems that stem from the lack of inservice training and from failure to provide incentives for goal-oriented behavior cannot be addressed through decision-making procedures. The best one can do in such a situation is to direct attention to the problem. Its resolution lies elsewhere.

A final limitation of this material is found in the differences in the statutes and policies of each state, which preclude the development of decision-making procedures with direct applicability across jurisdictions. Thus, the material presented here may require modifications to conform to regional differences. Also, since court decisions, such as those that deal with the placement of children in the least restrictive setting, affect worker behavior, and since these change over time, the material in this manual may have to be modified accordingly.

ORGANIZATION OF THE MANUAL

This manual is divided into three parts, each representing a different phase of the intake process. These phases are reception (Phase I), investigation and problem assessment (Phase II), and service planning (Phase III). The decisions made by workers in protective services and voluntary services are not the same. Protective service staff members must conduct an investigation to determine whether there is evidence of abuse or neglect. When evidence is found, the case is opened whether or not the family wants services. The decisions, in turn, that relate directly to the investigation are not of concern to staff members providing voluntary services. The decisions reviewed in each part of the manual are listed at the beginning of the section in which they are described. Whether they apply to protective services, voluntary services, or to both is shown.

Flow charts that show the process that workers follow to make decisions are presented for each decision covered. Questions that arise in the process of making each decision are bordered by diamonds. Directives for staff action are bordered by rectangles. The excerpt on page 10 from one of the flow charts illustrates how these are to be read.

When cases first come to reception, workers must determine the client's status in the agency. Whether the case is active is one of the first questions that an intake worker must address. If it is, a referral is made to the supervisor or worker handling the case. A negative answer to this question gives rise to a series of questions, as shown. The process followed by the intake worker will differ as a function of whether each of the remaining questions is answered affirmatively or negatively. Regardless of the answer, all courses of action shown in the flow charts culminate in a directive. Some directives result in closing the case as far as the agency is concerned; others draw attention to the next stage of the intake process. For example, when the question, Is the client eligible? is answered in the affirmative, workers are directed to document certain items of information and to refer the case for problem assessment.

In actual practice, the sequencing of decisions may differ from what is shown in this manual. Decisions are presented in a logical order reflecting the serial manner in which they are ordinarily made. However, certain choices—whether it is necessary to petition the court, for example—may be considered at several times, contingent upon the willingness of clients to work cooperatively with the agency and whether the client actually follows through with agreed-upon tasks. Some of the decisions that are covered may not reflect options available to workers. Policy or law may require workers to petition the court whenever there is evidence of abuse or neglect or whenever a child is removed from the care of her parents.

The forms that project workers used to record data for decision making

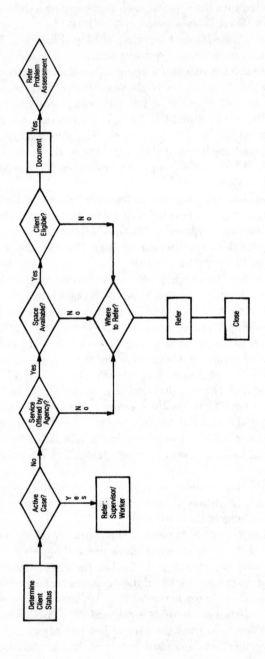

are presented in the manual. No attempt has been made to incorporate data elements that address agency administrative needs. These, too, vary considerably across settings. The focus was on developing forms for recording the data necessary to reach clinical decisions.

Finally, case examples are presented throughout the manual, as are tasks to enhance development of the learner's decision-making skills.

REFERENCES

1. Carol D. Austin. "Clinical Assessment in Context." *Social Work Research and Abstracts* 17 (Spring 1981).
2. Richard Bourne, and Eli H. Newberger. " 'Family Autonomy' or 'Coercive Intervention?' Ambiguity and Conflict in the Proposed Standards for Child Abuse and Neglect." In Richard Bourne and Eli H. Newberger (eds.), *Critical Perspectives on Child Abuse*. Lexington, MA: Lexington Books, 1979.
3. Scott Briar. "Clinical Judgment in Foster Care Placement." *Child Welfare* 42 (April 1963).
4. Donald Brieland. *An Experimental Study in the Selection of Adoptive Parents at Intake*. New York: Child Welfare League of America, 1959.
5. Rita Dukette. *Structured Assessment: A Decision Making Guide for Child Welfare*. U.S. Department of Health, Education and Welfare, Region V Office, Chicago, IL, n.d.
6. Arthur Emlen et al. *Overcoming Barriers to Planning for Children in Foster Care*. Portland, OR: Regional Research Institute for Human Services, Portland State University, 1977.
7. Naomi Golan. "How Caseworkers Decide: A Study of the Association of Selected Applicant Factors With Worker Decision in Admission Services." *Social Service Review* 43 (1969).
8. Joseph Goldstein, Anna Freud, and Albert J. Solnit. *Beyond the Best Interests of the Child*. New York: The Free Press, 1973.
9. Joseph Goldstein, Anna Freud, and Albert J. Solnit. *Before the Best Interests of the Child*. New York: The Free Press, 1979.
10. Roberta Gottesman. *The Child and the Law*. St. Paul, MN: West Publishing Co., 1981.
11. Institute of Judicial Administration, American Bar Association, Juvenile Justice Standards Project. *Standards Relating to Juvenile Records and Information Systems: Tentative Draft*. Cambridge, MA: Ballinger Publishing Co., 1977.
12. Irving L. Janis, and Leon Mann. *Decision Making: A Psychological Analysis of Conflict, Choice and Commitment*. New York: The Free Press, 1977.
13. *Legal Issues in Foster Care*. Raleigh, NC: National Association of Attorneys General, Committee on the Office of Attorney General, 1976.
14. Sheila R. Okpaku. "Psychology: Impediment or Aid in Child Custody Cases?" *Rutgers Law Review* 29 (1976).
15. Michael Phillips et al. *Factors Associated With Placement Decisions in Child Welfare*. New York: Child Welfare League of America, 1971.

16. Michael Phillips, Barbara L. Haring, and Ann W. Shyne. *A Model for Intake Decisions in Child Welfare.* New York: The Child Welfare League of America, 1972.
17. Victor Pike et al. *Permanent Planning for Children in Foster Care: A Handbook for Social Workers.* Portland, OR: Regional Research Institute for Human Services, Portland State University, 1977.
18. Carol M. Rose. *Some Emerging Issues in Legal Liability of Children's Agencies.* New York: Child Welfare League of America, 1978.
19. Ann W. Shyne, and Anita G. Schroeder. *National Study of Social Services to Children and Their Families.* Washington, D.C.: U.S. Department of Health, Education and Welfare, DHEW Publication No. (OHDS) 78–30150, 1978.
20. Arlene Skolnick. *The Intimate Environment: Exploring Marriage and the Family.* 2nd ed. Boston, MA: Little, Brown and Co., 1978.
21. Theodore J. Stein. "A Content Analysis of Social Caseworker and Client Interaction in Foster Care." Ph.D. diss., University of California, Berkeley, 1974.
22. Theodore J. Stein, and Eileen D. Gambrill. *Decision Making in Child Welfare: A Training Manual.* Berkeley, CA: University of California Extension Press, 1976.
23. Theodore J. Stein, Eileen D. Gambrill, and Kermit T. Wiltse. *Children in Foster Homes: Achieving Continuity of Care.* New York: Praeger Publishing Co., 1978. See for detailed review of the subject of decision making in child welfare.
24. Theodore J. Stein, and Tina Rzepnicki. "Decision Making in Child Welfare: Current Issues and Future Directions." In William Meezan and Brenda McGowan, *Child Welfare: Current Dilemmas—Future Directions*, in press.
25. Theodore J. Stein. "Child Welfare: New Directions in the Field and Their Implications for Education and Practice." *Journal of Education for Social Work*, in press.
26. Michael S. Wald. "Thinking About Public Policy Toward Abuse and Neglect of Children: A Review of Before the Best Interests of the Child." *Michigan Law Review* 78 (March 1980).
27. Sheldon H. White et al. *Federal Programs for Young Children: Review and Recommendations: Volume I: Goals and Standards of Public Programs for Children.* Washington, D.C.: Superintendent of Documents, 1973.
28. Kermit T. Wiltse. "Current Issues and New Directions in Foster Care." In *Child Welfare Strategy in the Coming Years.* Washington, D.C.: U.S. Department of Health, Education and Welfare, DHEW Publication No. (OHDS) 78–30158, 1978.
29. Martin Wolins. *Selecting Foster Parents.* New York: Columbia University Press, 1963.

Chapter One

PHASE I:
RECEPTION

GOAL

Determine Whether a Case *Seems* Appropriate
for Agency Services

DECISIONS

Protective Services   Is an Immediate Home Visit Necessary?

Voluntary Services   Should the Case be Referred for Problem
Assessment or Closed?

Both Services   Is Assistance Needed with the Investigation and Assessment?

RECEPTION IS the gateway to child welfare services. Cases reach this point through (1) reports of abuse or neglect, (2) client self-referral, or (3) referrals by community agencies. The goal of this phase of intake is to decide whether a case *seems* appropriate for agency services. Deciding whether a case *is* appropriate generally requires direct contact with clients in their own homes, which occurs during Phase II when the investigation and assessment stages of intake occur.

PROTECTIVE SERVICES AND VOLUNTARY SERVICES— DIFFERENCES AT RECEPTION

Protective services are almost always initiated by a third party report of abuse or neglect, rarely by the client. Since services are not voluntarily requested, their initiation constitutes an intrusion into family life. This can be justified if there is evidence that a child has been injured or is at risk of harm, and that protective action is necessary to safeguard the child.

To minimize interference in family life, protective service staff undertake an investigation (Phase II) to determine whether there is evidence that a child has been harmed or is in danger. If evidence is found, the case is opened whether or not the family wants assistance. Since voluntary services are initiated by clients or by referrals made with the client's knowledge, provision of service need not be justified by showing that it is necessary to protect children. Because staff who provide voluntary services do not undertake an investigation, the intake process requires fewer steps than in protective service.

Most states require an investigation each time there is a report of abuse or neglect [1]. This precludes closing cases at protective service reception unless there is insufficient information for follow-up. In contrast, cases may be closed at reception for voluntary services if the request is for information only, if the agency does not provide the service requested, if there is no space available in the service requested, or if clients do not meet eligibility requirements for entry into a program.

PROTECTIVE SERVICES

All states have laws that require certain persons with knowledge of abuse or neglect to report this information to a state agency that is designated as a reporting center. In general, doctors, social workers, teachers, and law enforcement personnel must file reports. Some jurisdictions mandate reporting by any person with knowledge of abuse or neglect. The locus for reporting differs across states. In most, reports are made to a division of the state department of social services. Some jurisdictions provide the option of reporting to a law enforcement agency [1].

Figure 1.1   **IS AN IMMEDIATE HOME VISIT NECESSARY?**

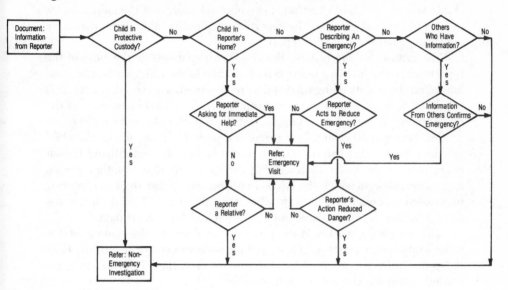

*The first decision at protective service reception is whether an immedi-ate home visit is necessary.** Generally, a period of 24 to 48 hours is allowed following receipt of a report for the investigation to begin. But there are situations in which the information provided by the reporter suggests that a child is in imminent danger and that warrant an immediate response, within an hour or two of the time a report is received.

Figure 1.1 shows the process that a protective service reception worker follows from the time that a report is received through the decision whether the situation warrants an emergency response.

The reception worker's *first task is to document* the information pro-vided by the reporter. This information is the basic data for determining whether an immediate home visit is necessary. Four categories of informa-tion are elicited from reporters.**

The subject family is identified by name, address, and telephone number; the age of the child who is the subject of the report is recorded, as is

---

*Occasionally, the child may not be in a home when an emergency visit is required, in which case the worker would go to wherever the child is located. This might happen, for instance, when the school makes a report that the child is afraid to go home.

**The data elements shown here are a sample of items recorded.

the parent's primary language. The reception worker asks for the name of the child's school, the child's teacher, the name and address of the family doctor or local clinic, and whether the reporter can identify others who may have information pertinent to the report.

The reason for the report, the child's whereabouts at the time of the report, when the incident being reported came to the caller's attention, and how often the events being reported were observed, are recorded next. It is important to learn whether the reporter has (1) first-hand knowledge of the events being described: for example, did the reporter observe a child being beaten, hear a child crying for a prolonged period of time, or did the child tell the reporter that she is afraid to return home? (2) second-hand knowledge, that is, the caller is describing events reported by another person (e.g., a neighbor) of which she has no firsthand knowledge; or (3) is reporting impressions, as might be the case when the caller says, "I think that something is wrong because I have not seen the child for several days."

The reception worker uses questions to discover the source of the caller's information, such as, Please tell me what you saw or heard? or, How did you acquire the information that you are reporting? Information is recorded, using direct quotes when possible.

The reporter is described next, including organizational affiliation if the person is a professional. Since the laws of many states allow reporters to remain anonymous, the reception worker may not be able to elicit information in this category. The reporter, however, may be the only person with first-hand knowledge of maltreatment, and the evidence that the reporter can offer can be crucial to sustaining allegations of abuse or neglect. The caller is thus told that his or her willingness to be identified and interviewed by the investigatory worker is important. A caller's wish to remain anonymous, however, must be respected.

Whether the reporter told the parents that a report was being made and, if so, how the parents responded, are the final items of information elicited.

Using Information for Decision Making

The information provided by the reporter must be reviewed and a decision made whether to respond immediately. The order in which information is elicited from reporters is important. Starting with identification of the subject family allows a protective service response should the caller have a "change of heart" and hang up the telephone before all the required information is obtained.

The child's whereabouts at the time of the report can determine whether immediate action is warranted. Children in protective custody are safe, precluding the need for immediate action. If the child is in the reporter's home and the reporter is asking that a representative of the agency pick up the youngster or says that the child is ill or injured, the worker knows that the case must be referred for an immediate home visit.

Whether the reporter is related to the child can have implications for deciding how quickly to respond. In some jurisdictions, if the reporter is a relative and is not asking for immediate help, state law permits the relative to retain custody of the child overnight. Immediate action is not required. In some states the child cannot remain in the reporter's home overnight unless the person is a relative or licensed foster parent. Familiarity with the laws of the state in which one is practicing is necessary to determine action under these conditions.

If the reporter is describing an emergency situation—for example, that she observed a child being beaten or heard a child's life being threatened— emergency action is warranted unless the reporter acts to reduce the emergency. For example, a reporter may call a child, who is playing in a dangerous area, indoors, or tell the child who cannot gain access to her own home to come into the reporter's home. Or, the caller may be willing to tell the child's parents what she observed. When the reporter describes an emergency situation, the receptionist asks the caller if she is willing to take action to reduce the danger reported if the action would not require the reporter to intervene between parent and child. Reporters should not be encouraged to act if they are hesitant to do so.

When the caller agrees to act, the reception worker states that he will call back in 15 to 20 minutes to learn what happened. If the danger has been reduced, a nonemergency response should suffice. Otherwise, a referral for immediate help is made.

There are situations in which the contents of the report suggest the need for immediate action but do not clearly indicate that this is necessary. The contents of the report may be impressionistic. The caller might say that she thinks that something is wrong because she has not seen the child for several days, or may report that the child appears to be ill or injured but be unable to describe the child's condition. The reception worker may not therefore be able to draw conclusions about the likelihood of danger.

Should this occur, an effort is made to contact others who may have information useful for decision making. If the family's physician or local clinic can be contacted, and if the child received medical attention, an immediate response may be avoided. Here, we assume that if the child were in danger, the medical person would have made the report and would not have released the youngster to her parents. Or, if school is in session, the youngster's teacher may be contacted to learn if the child attended class that day. If so, it is likely that injuries serious enough to require immediate attention would have been observed and reported.

If the reporter is describing events that took place several hours before the call was made, the question, Why have you waited until now to make this report? is asked. The answer to this question may determine the immediacy of response when the contents of the report are suggestive but not conclusive. If the caller's explanation for the delay seems reasonable, e.g., she says that she did not know what to do and just found out where to make the report, or states that she was not able to leave home to go to a phone booth because she was caring for her own children, the suggestion that immediate action is necessary is plausible.

But reporters may contradict themselves. A caller may describe a situation that appears to be an emergency and, at the same time, explain a delay by reporting that the situation did not seem urgent. Here, too, workers should contact others who may have relevant information.

When information from a reporter is inconclusive, and significant others cannot be contacted for additional information, workers must exercise professional judgment to determine whether an immediate response is needed. Since children may be at risk without medical attention, it may be best to err on the side of caution by initiating an immediate visit whenever a lay reporter describes a child who seems to be injured or ill, or who is in a situation that suggests possible danger.

Criteria for an Immediate Home Visit

(1) A reporter defines the situation as an emergency, and there is no contradictory information from other sources.

(2) A reporter provides information leading the reception worker to hypothesize that an emergency situation exists. For example, the reporter states that she observed a child being beaten; a child attempting to gain access to her own home; a child whose dress is inappropriate for the weather, so as to suggest that the youngster may become ill. Or, the reporter heard a child yelling or screaming for a prolonged period of time, or overheard a child being threatened by a caretaker or other person without a parent being present to whom the child can turn for help.

(3) A reporter states that a child has fled from home and is afraid to return, or a child makes a report and says that she is afraid to return home.

(4) If the situation reported suggests danger (for example, a child is playing in a heavily trafficked area where danger could be reduced if the child were called indoors), and the reporter has not indicated an unwillingness to speak with the parent or an inability to locate the parent, ask the reporter if she is willing to inform the parent of the child's situation. If yes, ask that she do so.

Ask the reporter is she would be willing to call the child indoors if a parent cannot be located. Tell the reporter that you will call back in 15 to 20 minutes to learn what happened. If the child is indoors, refer for a nonemergency investigation.

If the caller does not have a home phone, or if she cannot locate a parent or is not willing to try, and a young child can be heard crying or is observed to be in a dangerous situation, and if the caller told the child to come indoors or play elsewhere and the child will not listen, or the caller refuses to take action, the case should be referred for an immediate home visit.

Exceptions to Immediate Action

(1) A physician or qualified medical person can be reached by telephone, the child has received medical attention, and medical opinion is that an emergency response is not necessary.

(2) A youngster is of school age and the school can be contacted to learn if the child attended classes that day. If so, it is reasonable to assume that serious injuries would have come to the attention of a school authority. Even if they did not, the fact that the youngster went to school hints at the possibility that injuries are not so severe as to warrant immediate action.

(3) A person with firsthand information can be contacted (when the initial report was based on secondhand information) and the information provided indicates that an immediate visit is not necessary.

Bear in mind that an investigation occurs within 24 to 48 hours in nonemergency situations, and that older children are able to take certain actions in their own behalf.

VOLUNTARY CHILD WELFARE SERVICES

The reception worker's first task is to learn what service is being requested. Whether cases are closed at reception or continued for further assessment is determined in part by this information. Cases may be closed at this point if the client or referring source wants information only—for example, identifying information on community agencies offering assistance with marital problems or those providing day care services (fig. 1.2).

Unless the caller wants information only, the reception worker must determine the client's status in the agency. If the case is active, it is referred to the worker handling the case or to the worker's supervisor. When cases are transferred, the worker receiving it undertakes all remaining tasks otherwise completed by the reception worker, including denial of services for any of the following reasons: (1) The service requested may not be offered by the agency. Should this occur, the client is referred to an agency that offers the service. (2) There may not be any openings in the service re-

Figure 1.2 VOLUNTARY SERVICE RECEPTION—CLOSE OR REFER FOR ASSESSMENT?

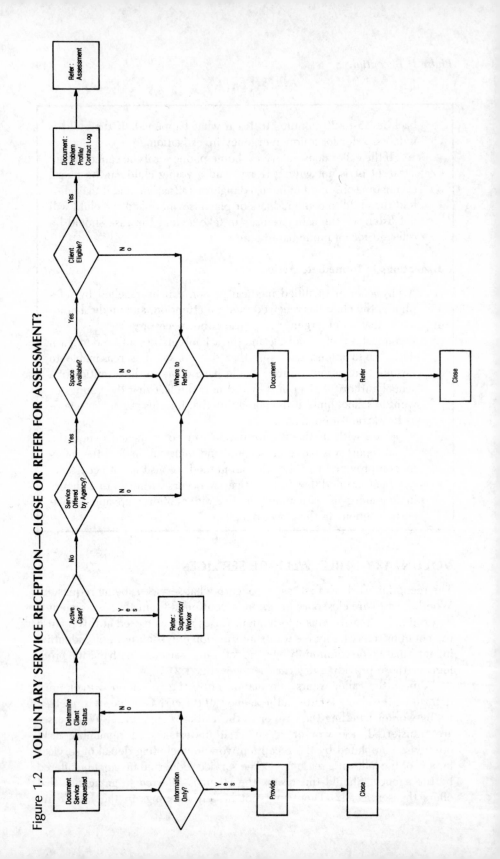

quested. For example, all of the slots in a day care program may be filled or all of the homemakers employed by the agency may be committed at the time the request is made. If the need for services is not urgent, the client may be put on a waiting list. When immediate help is required, referrals are made to other community agencies. (3) Clients may not meet eligibility requirements. Access to some services may be contingent upon whether the client is receiving other services. Whether one is receiving AFDC or is eligible for AFDC may be a precondition for receiving day care or homemaker services.

Determining the General Nature of the Presenting Problem and the Circumstances Surrounding Onset

Initial contact with voluntary service reception is made directly by clients or collateral resources. Thus, the reception worker is often able to obtain detailed information regarding client problems that receptionists at protective service are not able to acquire.*

The information that serves as a basis for deciding whether agency services will be offered and, if so, what these services will be, can be described at three levels. The first is general, consisting of the labels clients use to describe their problems, such as, "I am depressed, my child is unmanageable," and so forth. The second consists of examples of the behaviors, thoughts, and feelings that the client is referring to by the use of general labels and information regarding the circumstances surrounding the onset of the problem. (Illustrations appear below.) This information gives direction to the process of conducting an indepth assessment during which detailed information (level 3) needed to identify appropriate strategies for problem solving is gathered. This final level of information is compiled during the second phase of intake, when case assessment occurs. The following pages are devoted to the first and second levels of information.

The information may be recorded on a *problem profile* (fig. 1.3), which offers an overview of family difficulties as reported by clients and referring sources. The profile is begun at reception and will be completed during a home visit, when family members who did not participate in the initial interview may contribute examples of the problem or identify issues not noted during the interview.

Problems are numbered for the purpose of cross-referencing the information gathered at this time with information acquired at a later time. The

---

*The information-gathering activities described in the following pages are undertaken by protective service staff after the investigation is complete if there is evidence of maltreatment or risk.

Figure 1.3 **PROBLEM PROFILE**

Problem Number	Label	Who Labels	Who Has the Problem	Date	Examples	Situation	Assets
1.	diabetic	hospital records	Alice Hunt, age 13	5/13	1. hospitalized for acidosis weakness: diabetic 2. administers insulin irregularly	1. at home	1. knows how to take insulin
2.	blind	Sheila Hunt, mother	mother	5/13	1. can't see whether daughter takes insulin	1. at home	1. provides adequate child care in other areas
3.	inadequate housekeeping	worker	family	5/13	1. house is roach-infested	1. home	1. mother tries to keep house clean
4.	truant	school	Alice & Stanley Hunt (boy, age 14)	5/13	1. each child misses one or two days of school per week	1. Alice: when ill 2. Stanley: unknown	1. children do well in school

problems that necessitated the request for services are listed in the "Problem Label" column. The terminology used by the client or referring sources is used. The person who identifies the problem is noted next. This is important information because problems may be identified by different sources. For example, if a case is referred for services, the problem identified by the referring source is noted in the "Problem Label" column, the person referring the case is identified in the column headed "Who Labels," the client is listed in the next column, the date of the referral is then indicated, and efforts are made to elicit the information called for in the remaining columns. When more extensive information is needed at a later time, the data direct the worker to the most likely source.

Examples of the behaviors, thoughts, or feelings that define the client's problem are of critical importance. Different clients use similar words to refer to different problems. You must learn what a client means by being "depressed," or that her child is "unmanageable," and so forth.

Situations are identified for two reasons. First, many problems are situationally specific, occurring in certain contexts but not in others, or only in the presence of certain people. This information is necessary to direct attention to those situations in which additional information will be gathered during the assessment phase. It also directs worker attention to significant others who should be interviewed during assessment. The behavioral examples will serve as cues to focus worker attention during periods of observation. Identifying the situations where a problem occurs is one way in which clients may be helped to see that difficulties are not as pervasive as initially suggested. In the "Assets" column the worker lists strengths that the client identifies in relation to each problem cited, thus placing family difficulties in perspective by balancing the problem view with whatever positive information is provided. As will be seen, this is useful when the final decision, whether to provide services or to make a referral, is made.

Additional Information

In addition to the information described above, reception staff members acquire demographic data on the family as well as information regarding the client's current and prior use of services. (See pp. 67–72.) When case assessment is discussed later, information from other service providers can contribute to decisions regarding whether services are offered, and if so, what services are most likely to benefit the family.

Detailed service data—for example, who provided services, what specific problems were addressed, how these were addressed, and information regarding client progress in service programs—will be gathered at a later time.

All contacts made with and in behalf of clients should be recorded in a *case log* (fig. 1.4). When voluntary services are requested, the log is begun at

Figure 1.4 CLIENT CONTACT LOG

Family Name	Date of Appointment	Type of Contact	Place	Time	Person(s) in Attendance	Purpose	Results
Hunt	5/13	in-person:	client's home	11 A.M.	Mrs. Helen Hunt	elicit information re. service request	completed problem profile
					Alice Hunt		arranged to speak with Alice's physician & children in school

reception. Protective service workers begin case logs when they make a first home visit, or when they make contacts with collaterals to gather information prior to a home visit. The log is maintained as long as the family is served by the agency. The information recorded provides a running account of all transactions between staff members and clients, collaterals, and significant others, such as relatives, friends, and neighbors of the family. Appointments made and whether they are kept are recorded.

The problem profile and case log are transferred to a unit supervisor who assigns the case to a worker for a home visit and continuation of case assessment. When the assessment process is completed, a final decision whether to open the case is made. The tasks undertaken during the assessment are described in Chapter 2.

Is Assistance Needed With Assessment or Investigative Tasks?

Many of the clients served by child welfare agencies have problems whose assessment is beyond the skills of one person. The expertise of medical personnel, attorneys, psychologists, and psychiatrists, in addition to those of the child welfare worker, may be needed to determine the exact nature of client problems and to select appropriate interventions (fig. 1.5). Thus, whether or not assistance is needed with the initial investigation must be decided. The decision whether or not to request assistance with case assessment confronts workers in both protective and voluntary services. This decision may be made at protective services reception or by the worker who will

Figure 1.5 **IS ASSISTANCE REQUIRED: ASSESSMENT/INVESTIGATION?**

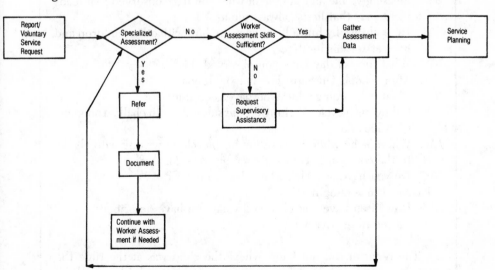

initiate the investigation. For example, if a reporter states that a child has
been injured, a worker may ask that a public health nurse accompany him on
the home visit to examine the child and to determine whether medical
attention is necessary. A relatively inexperienced worker in either protective
or voluntary services may request assistance with basic investigatory procedures with which he is unfamiliar. The decision to request assistance may be
made at a later time. Based on observations made during a first home visit, a
worker may ask for diagnostic assistance from a psychologist or may determine that it is necessary to take the child for a physical examination.

   This decision may be reconsidered at later stages of a case, based on the
worker's observations and information provided during a home visit. Supervisory approval should be obtained before involving others in the assessment
process.

FOR DISCUSSION

1. The Evans family came to the attention of protective services in
March, 1981 when a neighbor telephoned the reporting center regarding Gregory Evans, age 7. Identifying information on the family was
obtained. The following dialogue illustrates the exchange of information between the reception worker (RW) and the reporter (R) about
why the report was being made.

RW: What is the reason for making this report?
  R: Everyday I see that child by himself. He is always alone.
RW: Please give me an example of what you have observed that leads
      you to say that he is "always alone."
  R: He is always by himself. I never see him with other children and
      I never see his mother.
RW: What time of day have you observed this?
  R: After school. On Saturday, maybe Sunday.
RW: What is he doing when you have seen him?
  R: Riding his bicycle. Writing on the sidewalk with chalk. You know
      what kids do.
RW: Where is he when he is riding his bicycle or writing with chalk?
  R: In the courtyard. Down the street. Who knows?
RW: Do you have any idea where his mother is?
  R: No. I never see her.
RW: How often have you observed what you have described?
  R: All the time. Everyday.

   The reporter did not know where the child was at the time the
report was made. She would not give her name and did know where

Gregory went to school. She had never discussed her observations with the mother.

TASK ONE

State your decision and the rationale for it.

2. On April 17, 1981, at 5:30 A.M., a nurse from County Hospital telephoned protective service reception. A Mrs. Clybourne had brought her 2-year-old daughter into the hospital's emergency room with a broken right arm. The mother was said to be "verbally incoherent," e.g., she did not seem to understand the questions asked by the doctor nor was she able to complete a sentence. Rather, her verbalizations wandered from one thought to another. Moreover, the examining physician had noticed "track marks" on the mother's arm. She was detained for an examination.

The fact that there were other children at home (number and ages could not be determined) was the only exact information elicited from the mother. Her address was obtained from a driver's license. There was no telephone number listed for the family.

TASK TWO

State your decision and the rationale for it.

DECISIONS AND RATIONALE

EXAMPLE 1: RECEPTION

Decision Refer case for investigation: nonemergency.

Rationale The reporter did not describe an emergency situation, nor did the information provided suggest an emergency to the reception worker. In fact, the situation reported might be more normative than unusual.

EXAMPLE 2: RECEPTION

Decision Refer for immediate investigation.

Rationale There were other children at home. Since the mother was not able to provide information—for example, whether the children were being supervised—and since there was no telephone, the suggestion that the children were in immediate danger is plausible.

REFERENCES

1. *Trends in Child Protection Laws—1979.* Denver, CO: Education Commission of the States, October, 1979.

Chapter Two

PHASE II: INVESTIGATION AND PROBLEM ASSESSMENT

GOAL

Determine Whether a Case Is Appropriate for Agency Services

DECISIONS

Protective Services   Is a Child in Immediate Danger?

-if so-

Can the Child be Safeguarded at Home or Is Protective Custody Necessary?
Is There Credible Evidence of Abuse or Neglect?

Voluntary Services   Is the Family Eligible for Voluntary Services?

Both Services   What Are the Specific Problems in Need of Resolution?
Is Out-of-Home Placement Necessary?

-if so-

What Is the Most Appropriate Placement Facility?
Is It Necessary to Petition the Court?

THE GOAL OF this phase of intake is to decide whether a case is appropriate for agency services. In protective services, reaching this decision involves more steps than in voluntary programs since protective service personnel must conduct an investigation to determine whether there is credible evidence of abuse or neglect.*

Finding credible evidence is a sufficient basis for opening a case to the agency.** Having decided to open a case, protective service personnel conduct an assessment of family life to identify the exact problems that must be resolved to reduce or eliminate risk of further maltreatment. Staff in voluntary programs conduct an assessment to identify family problems and determine whether services will be offered by the agency or the family referred elsewhere. The assessment process is similar for both services.

The process workers follow in conducting an investigation is described in the first part of this chapter. Three decisions common to protective and voluntary programs—(1) Is out-of-home care necessary? (2) What is the most appropriate placement facility? (3) Is it necessary to petition the court?—are reviewed in this section because they arise during the investigation.

THE INVESTIGATION

When the investigation begins, the worker's foremost concern is with the safety of each child in the home. If there is evidence of danger, it must be determined whether children can be safeguarded at home or must be taken into protective custody. The issues that concern protective service staff in reaching these decisions are shown in figure 2.1.

The worker responsible for the investigation receives the information that was recorded by the reception worker, including an indication whether an immediate home visit is necessary. If immediate action is called for and assistance with the investigation is needed, a request for aid must be put forth.

Information from a variety of sources can contribute to the decisions made during the investigation. Some information can be gathered before the first home visit if immediate action is not required; other information cannot be obtained until the worker meets with the family. In the former category is information logged in the state's central registry, such as previous reports on the family, data found in agency files, and information from collateral resources whose names were given to the reception worker or whose names appear in case records.

---

*Credible evidence, as defined in Illinois law, for example, is information that would lead a reasonable person to believe that the facts and circumstances would support an allegation of abuse or neglect.

**This does not mean that cases in all agencies will necessarily be opened. In Illinois, for example, workers have the alternative of "founding" a case, e.g., logging it on the central registry as a case in which evidence of maltreatment was present, and not opening the case if there is reason to question the value of providing services.

All of the services that a family has used or is currently using may not be identified in records. Since information from service providers can contribute to decision making, workers will question family members to learn about resources used.

The following illustrates how information that is retrieved from records or gained from collaterals can influence decisions made. From information gathered during the investigation it is not always possible to determine conclusively whether a child has been harmed or is in danger. For example, a worker responding to a report that a young child is not being supervised may find a parent at home when he arrives. The child may be unharmed and the parent may deny having left the youngster alone. If the substance of the report cannot be confirmed, there may be no choice but to close the case. But if there are prior confirmed reports similar in nature to the report under investigation, these can strengthen a weak case since they suggest a pattern of supervisorial neglect. It is important to know whether your state expunges unconfirmed reports. If not, information logged in the central registry may have little usefulness for decision making. Previous reports may reflect attempts by people to harass a family that does not conform to community standards but whose behavior is not harmful to children.

Collateral resources may have knowledge of a family that is useful for decision making. A mental health counselor may have diagnostic information showing that a child is suffering from emotional problems. The counselor's records may indicate that the child's parents have not followed through with a recommended plan for treatment. This information could be used to support a claim that the youngster is being emotionally neglected or abused.

Note that in both examples the suggestion that a child has been mistreated takes into account parental actions as well as the child's situation or condition. If the parent of an unsupervised child arranged for child care or accepted a worker's help in making arrangements, or the parent whose child has emotional problems followed a recommended treatment plan, there would not be a basis for alleging neglect or abuse.

A worker begins the investigation by describing to the family the nature of the report (while maintaining the confidentiality of the reporting source) and the state law that requires the investigation. If entry to the home is denied, action must be taken that will result in observing and speaking to the parents and children, since the question, Are the children safe? must be answered. The action taken depends on state law. Some jurisdictions require that a warrant be obtained to gain entry to the home. In others, police and/or social service personnel are empowered to enter the home without a warrant when they are responding to a report of maltreatment.

The conditions under which the investigation takes place are often strained. Parents may be nervous or frightened when apprised of the report, whether or not they have mistreated their child. If a child has been abused

Figure 2.1 IS CHILD IN DANGER? CAN CHILD BE SAFEGUARDED AT HOME OR IS PROTECTIVE CUSTODY NECESSARY?

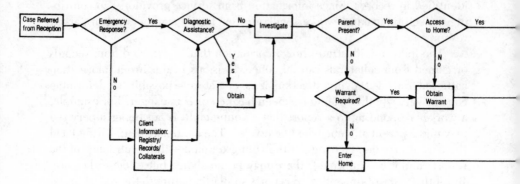

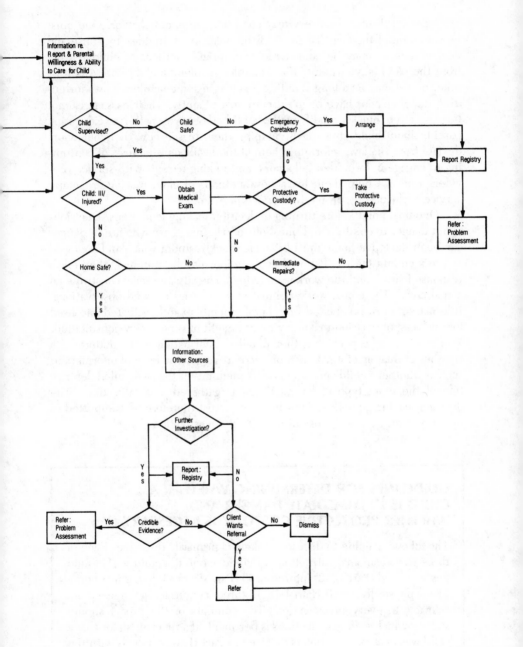

or neglected, fear of discovery may condition parental behavior. One must be cognizant of the fact that some of the behaviors forbidden by abuse and neglect statutes may be considered appropriate methods of child rearing from the parents' viewpoint. For example, spanking a child with a belt or other object may be a long-standing practice in some families. Laws forbidding such behavior have been enacted only recently. Their passage cannot be expected to quickly modify well-established behavior patterns. Educating parents about child abuse laws, helping them to see how their behaviors deviate from the law, informing them of the legal consequences of continuing to engage in forbidden behaviors, and linking parents with service providers who can help them learn new methods of child rearing are major services provided by protective service personnel.

One final point before turning to decision-making guidelines. Decisions about danger to children and questions of whether those who are in danger can be protected at home must be made quickly, under what can be viewed as crisis circumstances. Parental cooperation may be minimal, the child's response fearful, and the worker uninvited. The situation may constitute an actual crisis. Therefore, workers must make a series of rapid observations. Information must be elicited from family members and evaluated and used for on-the-spot decision making without benefit of supervisory consultation. Workers cannot expect to gather detailed information or to undertake a rigorous evaluation of it. At best, one acquires a general level of information, such as whether a child appears to be harmed, rather than a detailed description of the exact type of harm. Detail is gathered at a later time. The decision-making guidelines presented here must therefore be committed to memory if they are to be useful during the investigation.

GUIDELINES FOR DETERMINING WHETHER A CHILD IS IN IMMEDIATE DANGER AND WHETHER PROTECTIVE CUSTODY IS NECESSARY

The following guide to decision making is primarily directive. Each of three parts contains instructions to guide action if a child is (1) found unsupervised (Part I), (2) injured or ill (Part II), or (3) living in a home that is physically unsafe (Part III). All three sections are not necessarily relevant to every investigation. The contents of the report should suggest which section or sections is pertinent. If a reporter states that a child was beaten, attention is directed to Part II, which deals with the child's physical condition. Questions regarding supervision and conditions of the home are not then of immediate concern.

PART I. SUPERVISION

1. *IS THERE AN ADULT IN THE HOME?*

    (a) If NO, go to question 2.

    (b) If YES, determine the caretaker's relationship to the child. If the caretaker is not the child's parent ask whether she is in the home by arrangement with the parent, whether she is willing to provide care until the parent returns home, and when the parent is expected home. Ask where the parent is and obtain a telephone number where the parent can be reached, if possible.

    (c) Does the caretaker seem able to care for the child? (Is her speech coherent? Is the caretaker able to discuss the child's supervision or does her train of thought wander, as evidenced by incomplete sentences and difficulties in understanding what you are saying—assuming that difficulties are not a function of language differences?)

    (d) If the caretaker is the child's parent and seems unable to care for the child but will accept help, ask if there is a neighbor or relative you might call to provide assistance. If so, arrange for help. If not, send an emergency caretaker into the home. If the caretaker is not the child's parent, is not able to care for the youngster or is unwilling to do so, try to locate a parent by telephone or by going to nearby homes. If the parent is located, ask that she return home immediately. Unless the parent returns while you are there, send an emergency caretaker into the home. If the caretaker is not able to provide care, if she will not accept help, or if emergency caretaker services are not available, take the child into protective custody.

    (e) If the caretaker is not a parent but is able and willing to care for the child and is in the home by arrangement with the parent, there is no reason to assume danger. The parent should be informed of the report. Further action is not warranted unless there are previous reports regarding supervision.

    (f) If the parent or caretaker prevents you from seeing the child, explain that, by law, you will have to request police assistance to determine whether the child is all right. If the parent or caretaker still refuses to let you see the youngster, enlist the aid of a police officer. Further action will be contingent upon what you observe in relation to the condition of the child and the home. (See Parts II and III.*)

(g) If the parent or caretaker is verbally nonresponsive and/or physically unable to move, call for emergency medical assistance. Take the child into protective custody.

(h) If the parent or caretaker is bedridden but is able to discuss the child's supervision and condition, ask how the youngster is being supervised, fed, sent to school, and so forth. Inquire into the nature of the caretaker's illness and whether she has received medical attention.

   (1) If the parent or caretaker seems able to provide supervision—for example, she can observe the child at play, is able to get out of bed should the child need help, is able to feed the child or the child is able to feed herself, and there is food in the house (or if you can obtain food)—further action at this time is not warranted. A return visit within 48 hours to see how the family is managing is called for.

   (2) Absent these conditions, have arrangements been made for a neighbor or relative to provide aid? If so, ask for permission to speak with the person to confirm her willingness to help. If the parent or caretaker will not cooperate, tell her that you will have to take the child into protective custody. If you can confirm the availability of help, further action is not warranted.

   (3) If help has not been arranged, is there a relative or neighbor who can come to the home to provide assistance or to whose home the child can be brought? If so, and the parent or caretaker is agreeable to your making arrangements for help, do so.

   (4) If a caretaker is not available, or help is not accepted, the child should be taken into protective custody.

   (5) If the parent or caretaker has not received medical attention, ask if she would like you to arrange for it.

2. *DID YOU FIND AN INFANT ALONE?*

   (a) If NO, go to question 3.

   (b) If YES, try to locate a parent by asking a neighbor. If a parent is

---

*If a parent is not cooperative, but the child is being supervised and her physical condition and conditions of the home do not suggest a problem, there are probably no reasonable grounds for further action.

located or can be contacted by telephone, arrange for immediate supervision.

(c) If a parent cannot be found, ask the neighbor if she would be willing to supervise the infant until the parent returns home. Unless the neighbor is a relative or licensed foster parent, emergency supervision should not last overnight unless the person is willing to stay with the child in the child's home. If you arrange for supervision, give the neighbor/relative a telephone number where you or an agent of the agency can be reached.

(d) If immediate supervision cannot be arranged, send an emergency caretaker into the home. Otherwise, take the infant into protective custody.

3. *WAS A PRESCHOOL CHILD FOUND ALONE?*

(a) If NO, go to question 4.

(b) If YES, ask the child if she knows how to locate her parent or if she was given instructions about what to do if help is needed.

(c) If the child has instructions, for example, to contact a nearby relative or neighbor, you should telephone that person or go to that home to learn about the child care arrangements made.

(d) If an adult is located, arrange for immediate supervision. Otherwise, send an emergency caretaker into the home or, if none is available, take the child into protective custody.

4. *WAS A SCHOOL-AGE CHILD FOUND ALONE?*

(a) If NO, go to question 5.

(b) If YES, follow the instructions under question 3, b and c.

(c) If an adult cannot be located, but the child is inside the home, or has access to the home, ask the child if she knows when the parent is expected home and if she minds being alone until the parent returns.

(d) If the child has access to the indoors, knows when a parent will return, and does not express fear at being alone, ask the child what she would do if a fire started, if she felt ill, or became fearful. If the child has the telephone number of a family physician or nearby clinic, an emergency number such as 911, or was told to dial the operator to ask for help, an hypothesis of immediate danger is not warranted.

Give the youngster a telephone number where you or other agency representatives can be reached. Tell the child to telephone you if her parent does not return. Leave a note for

the parent describing why you were at the home and instruct-
ing the parent to telephone you as soon as she returns. Indicate
your intention to return to the home if a call is not received.
Emergency action can be deferred.

(e) If the youngster is afraid to be alone or if there is no phone in
the home or nearby neighbor to whom the child can turn for
help, send an emergency caretaker into the home. Otherwise,
take the child into protective custody.

(f) If the parent does not telephone you as instructed, a return
home visit is called for. If the child is still alone, send an
emergency caretaker into the home. Otherwise, take the child
into protective custody.

5. *WAS A YOUNG CHILD LEFT IN THE CARE OF AN OLDER
SIBLING?*

(a) If NO, go to Part II, Child's Condition.

(b) If YES, follow through with the instructions for locating a parent under question 3, b and c. If a parent cannot be located, but
the child knows when her parent will return, a dangerous situation should not be assumed.

(c) The older child's self-help skills should be assessed in the manner suggested under item d, question 4. The instructions under
e and f, question 4, should be followed.

PART II. CHILD'S CONDITION

1. *DID YOU OBSERVE BURNS, LACERATIONS, BRUISES,
WELTS, OR OTHER SIGNS OF INJURY ON THE CHILD'S
BODY?*

-or-

2. *DOES A CHILD APPEAR TO BE ILL, E.G., IS SHE IN BED? IS
SHE FEVERISH?*

-or-

3. *DID A CHILD TELL YOU THAT SHE IS IN PAIN?*
Negative answers to these questions should direct your attention to
the child's overt behavior for clues to whether there may be internal
injuries. Internal injuries should affect the child's ability to talk,
play, or move about when asked to.

(a) If NO to these questions, go to Part III, Conditions of the Home.

(b) If YES to any of these questions, is there evidence that the
child has received medical attention? Evidence could take the

form of a statement from a parent that a child was seen by a physician or public health nurse; bandages applied to a wound; a prescription with the child's name, bearing a date that corresponds to the investigation/report and/or written instructions from a medical person as to how the parent is to minister to the child.

(c) If the parent says that the child has received medical attention, obtain the name, address, and telephone number of the medical person or clinic where the child was seen. Ask the parent's permission to contact the person or facility for information on the child's illness or injury.

(d) If the parent will not provide this information or refuses permission for you to contact the medical person, she should be told that, under law, you will have to arrange for an immediate medical examination.

If you have the name of a medical person, contact should be made as soon as possible. Further protective action will depend upon the information you receive. If information from a medical person confirms the parent's report, and there is no suggestion that the injury was deliberately inflicted, further action is not warranted.

If the medical report differs from that of the parent, ask what the physician or nurse thinks needs to be done. We must assume that if the injury or illness were life threatening, or if there were evidence of deliberate intent to harm, the child would not have been released to the parent. Therefore, a hypothesis of immediate danger is not warranted.

(e) If there is no evidence that the child has received medical attention, is there evidence that the parent has ministered to the child? For example, has salve been applied to a burn? Is there a bandage on a wound? Does the parent state that she is giving a child aspirin to bring down a fever?

(f) If the parent is attending to the child's illness and the child does not appear to be seriously ill (for instance, the child is able to speak to you in a manner that is coherent for her age, or is sitting up in bed playing with toys or watching television), emergency action is not called for. However, if the parent does not have a family doctor or access to medical facilities (and a Medicaid card, if appropriate), the name, address, and telephone number of the nearest clinic, hospital, or public health facility should be provided. If the parent wishes, arrangements should be made for a public health nurse to visit the home or for transportation to take the child to a medical facility for an examination.

(g) If the child has not received medical attention and/or the parent has not made an effort to minister to the child, and, in your best judgment, the injury or illness seems serious, arrange for immediate medical attention.

4. *IF THE CHILD HAS BEEN INJURED, IMMEDIATE MEDICAL ATTENTION IS CALLED FOR REGARDLESS OF THE SEVERITY OF THE INJURY IF:*

(a) The parent will not explain how an injury was sustained.

(b) The parent's and child's explanation differ.

(c) The parent's explanation is not congruent with your observations—for example, you are told that lacerations on a child's back are the result of an accident.

(d) The child is so withdrawn that she will not respond to your questions and will not approach you or her parent.

(1) The parent should be asked to take the child to the nearest clinic or emergency room immediately. A representative of the agency should accompany the parent. If the parent will not take the child for an examination, the child should be taken into protective custody and examined by a medical person. Further action would depend upon the outcome of the medical examination.

5. *THE CHILD SHOULD BE TAKEN INTO PROTECTIVE CUSTODY FOLLOWING A MEDICAL EXAMINATION IF:*

(a) There is evidence that physical abuse or nutritional neglect is so severe as to be life threatening.

(b) There was an intent to kill the child, even if an injury is not severe, as evidenced by poisoning or assault with a deadly weapon, or if a child was repeatedly beaten with an object.

(c) There is evidence of abuse or neglect that, if not attended to, can be hypothesized to threaten the child's life, and the parent refuses help.

(d) There is medical evidence of repeated abuse. For example, X-rays show previous injuries that were not medically treated and that a medical person suggests could not have been sustained by accident.

(e) There is any recurrence of severe abuse or neglect after services were offered.

(f) There is psychiatric or psychological evidence of extreme behavioral disturbance or withdrawal by the child, and the parent rejects the child.

(g) Evidence suggests that the parent is not competent. For instance, a medical person states that the parent does not understand instructions for ministering to the child (assuming that nonunderstanding is not a function of language differences), and there are no resources, such as family, friends, or emergency caretaker/homemaker services to help in the home where an assessment is undertaken.

(h) A child has been raped by a related adult or nonrelated adult known to the parent and the parent did not attempt to protect the child.

PART III. CONDITIONS OF THE HOME

1. The following list describes conditions of the family home that require action by protective services.

   (a) The outside temperature is below 50° F. and there is no heat in the home.

   (b) There are broken windows with jagged edges of glass.

   (c) There is exposed electrical wiring.

   (d) Bathroom facilities are not in working order.

   (e) There are rotten floorboards in the home.

   (f) There are holes in the roof through which rain or snow can enter.

   (g) There is garbage/feces in the home which, in your opinion, pose a health hazard.

   (h) There are rats in the home.

Any of these conditions may pose a threat to the entire family. Neglect should not be assumed unless the parent owns the home and refuses to make affordable repairs, or unless the parent refuses assistance from the agency. Efforts should be made to have repairs undertaken or to relocate the entire family. The child should be removed if the parent will not cooperate.

If repairs can be made immediately or before the point at which they are likely to cause danger (for example, a broken furnace can be repaired before winter), arrangements for the repairs should be made. Follow up to ensure that necessary repairs were made.

If conditions cannot be improved in time to avert danger, the parent should be asked if there is a neighbor or relative with whom the family can stay until repairs are made or new housing found. If there are no safe alternatives for the entire family, the child should be placed in an emergency shelter until alternative living arrangements can be made for the entire family.

Worker observations in the three areas reviewed above are summarized on a checklist (fig. 2.2) immediately after the home visit, before specific facts are forgotten or modified by memory. If protective custody was undertaken, the reasons are also indicated on the checklist. The ways in which workers determine what further action, if any, is necessary, are reviewed later in this section.

Figure 2.2   **CHECKLIST: OBSERVATIONS FROM FIRST HOME VISIT**

INSTRUCTIONS   Record your observations on the following checklist by checking yes or no to each item. If a child was taken into protective custody, indicate why in Part IV. Use the narrative section at the end to summarize your observations, clarify your actions and recommend further steps (e.g., arrange for psychological testing, request information from collaterals). If your observations suggest that the investigation should be closed, place a checkmark in the box to the left. Explain your reasoning in the narrative.

☐

PART I. SUPERVISION

	YES	NO
1. Supervision was an issue?	____	____
(a) If NO, go to Part II: Child's Condition	____	____
2. If YES: Was there a caretaker in the home?	____	____
(a) What is the caretaker's relationship to the child?		
_____		
(b) If not a parent, was the caretaker there by arrangement with a parent?	____	____
(c) Regardless of relationship, was the caretaker able to supervise the child?	____	____
(d) Regardless of relationship, was the caretaker willing to supervise the child?	____	____
3. Did you find a caretaker who was bedridden?	____	____
(a) If YES, was the caretaker able to care for the child?	____	____
(b) If the caretaker could not care for the child, was there a neighbor or relative who was willing to provide child care?	____	____
4. Did you find a caretaker whose verbal or nonverbal behavior made it impossible for you to discuss the child's supervision?	____	____

5. Was the caretaker cooperative? _____ _____

6. Did you find an infant alone? _____ _____

7. Did you find a preschool age child alone? _____ _____

8. Was the child able to care for herself? (briefly explain in the narrative). _____ _____

9. Did you find a young child being supervised by an older sibling? _____ _____

PART II. CHILD'S CONDITION

                                                                        YES   NO

1. Was the child's condition an issue? _____ _____

2. If NO, go to Part III, Condition of the Home.

3. If YES, did you observe an injured child (e.g., one with burns, lacerations, bruises, etc.)? _____ _____
   (a) If YES, use the narrative section to report the caretaker's and child's explanation of how injuries were sustained.

4. Did you observe a child who appeared to be ill? _____ _____

5. Did a child tell you that she is in pain? _____ _____

6. Did the child's overt behavior seem limited (e.g., the child was unable to move a limb or turn her head)? _____ _____
   (a) If YES to 4, 5, or 6, use the narrative section to describe what you observed or were told.

7. Is there evidence to suggest that the child has received medical attention? (If YES, describe the evidence in the narrative section.) _____ _____
   (a) Insert the name, address, and telephone number of the medical person or clinic.

   _____

   (b) Is the caretaker's report congruent with the medical report? _____ _____
       (1) If NO, use the narrative section to describe the discrepancy.

8. Is there evidence to suggest that the caretaker has ministered to the child's medical needs? _____ _____
   (a) If YES, describe the evidence in the narrative.

PART III. CONDITIONS OF THE HOME

                                                                        YES   NO

1. Was a condition of the home an issue? _____ _____
   If NO, go to Part IV, Protective Custody.

2. If YES, was the outside temperature below 50 degrees F without heat in the home? _____ _____

3. Were there broken windows with jagged edges of glass? _____ _____
4. Was there exposed electrical wiring? _____ _____
5. Were there indoor/outdoor bathroom facilities in working order? _____ _____
6. Were there rotten floorboards that would pose danger to a child? _____ _____
7. Were there holes in the roof through which rain or snow could enter? _____ _____
8. Was there garbage/feces in the home that you think pose a health hazard? _____ _____
9. Were there rats in the home? _____ _____
10. OTHER: Were there any issues not covered in Parts I through II that in your opinion pose danger to a child? If YES, use the narrative section to describe the condition and your reason for presuming danger. _____ _____

PART IV. DID YOU TAKE PROTECTIVE CUSTODY OF A CHILD?

YES   NO

If YES, check which of the following reasons apply. If more than one reason is applicable, please rank the reasons in order of their importance by inserting number 1 in the space next to the most important reason, number 2 in the space next to the second most important reason, and so forth.

1. No caretaker able to care for child. _____
2. No caretaker willing to care for child. _____
3. Caretaker unable to care for child and no relatives or neighbors available to help. _____
4. Caretaker would not accept help. _____
5. Emergency services (e.g., homemaker, emergency caretaker) not available. _____
6. Child abandoned. _____
7. Child unable to care for self. _____
8. Child injured; caretaker would not explain how injury occurred. _____
9. Location or type of injury suggests abuse and parent's explanation conflicts with observations. _____
10. Child's explanation conflicts with caretaker's explanation. _____
11. Child said that she is afraid to stay at home. _____
12. Child appears to be seriously ill and parent will not arrange for medical examination or will not allow you to arrange for an examination. _____

13. Medical evidence of previous injuries where the location or type of injury suggests abuse. _____

14. Medical evidence of previous injuries that did not receive medical attention, and medical opinion is that the injuries could not have been sustained by accident. _____

15. The type of location of the injury (burns on an infant's buttocks, whipmarks) suggest an intention to harm the child. _____

16. Home unsafe, relocation of family not possible, and immediate repairs cannot be made. _____

17. Other (use narrative section to describe other reasons for taking protective custody). _____

NARRATIVE

DETERMINING WHETHER THERE IS CREDIBLE EVIDENCE OF ABUSE OR NEGLECT

Possible outcomes of the first home visit are (1) closing the case when there is no basis for continuing the investigation, referring clients for assistance when requested; (2) opening case if there is credible evidence of abuse or neglect; or (3) continuing the case for further investigation. In this section we review the process workers follow to determine which course of action to take by examining (a) sources of information that contribute to decision making, (b) the different types of evidence workers gather, and (c) how information is used to determine whether there is evidence of maltreatment.

To begin, it is extremely important that workers familiarize themselves with the statutes of the state in which they practice. The conditions that constitute abuse or neglect differ across jurisdictions. Equally important is learning about the kinds of evidence required to substantiate an allegation of maltreatment. In Illinois, for example, psychological and/or psychiatric reports are needed to support charges of emotional abuse or neglect. Medical reports are required whenever physical abuse or nutritional neglect is an issue.

Sources of Information

Sources of information that contribute to decision making are listed in figure 2.3. The process workers follow in reaching a determination of credible evidence and whether to open a case for services is depicted in figure 2.4.

Information from a variety of sources may contribute to decision making, as should be clear from a review of data sources listed in figure 2.3. It is equally clear that allegations of maltreatment or the suggestion that a child is at risk carry the implication that parents intended to harm a child or that they refused to correct conditions creating risk, whether through use of their own resources or by using the resources of social agencies.

When credible evidence is provided by a reporter, the basic goal of the investigation is met. The information given to the reception worker is logged in the central registry. A protective service worker will visit the family, inform them of the report, describe the evidence, explain the law, and review the implications of the report for the family. In most states a minimum implication is that the family will have to accept services in order to reduce the likelihood of future child maltreatment. In some jurisdictions criminal charges may be filed if, for example, there is evidence of sexual abuse or if physical abuse was life-threatening. A child may be taken into

---

Figure 2.3   **SOURCES OF INFORMATION FOR DETERMINING WHETHER THERE IS CREDIBLE EVIDENCE OF ABUSE OR NEGLECT**

A determination of credible evidence may be made using information:

1. *Provided by a Reporter.* Credible evidence may exist at the time a report is made. For example, a medical person may have evidence that a child has

been injured and medical opinion may hold that the injury could not have been sustained by accident.

-or-

A reporter may have observed a child being beaten and may be willing to testify to that effect.

2. *Provided by a Parent* who acknowledges an act of abuse or neglect.

3. *Provided by a Child* who states that she was beaten or reports some form of sexual abuse or molestation.

4. *Provided by Psychiatric or Psychological Consultants* who have tested a child and whose opinion it is that the child is suffering from emotional problems or is at risk of such problems, *and* the parent rejects the child and/or refuses assistance when offered.

5. *Provided by School Personnel* whose records show repeated absences, *and* there is evidence that the parent is deliberately keeping the child from attending school.

6. *Credible Evidence May Come from Worker Observations.* One may observe a parent who is not able to care for a child and refuses to accept help. Consequently, the child may be taken into protective custody. A description of worker observations and parental responses may be sufficient to sustain an allegation of maltreatment.

-or-

a. Information provided by a reporter coupled with that gained during an interview with parents and others may support allegations of maltreatment. Conflicts between a parent's and a child's explanation of how an injury was sustained, between a parent's report and medical evidence, or between information provided by the parent and the type or location of an injury may permit inferences as to how the injury was sustained.

-or-

b. Worker observations coupled with previous information may yield credible evidence. If one finds an unsupervised child, even though immediate danger does not exist, the fact that there are previous confirmed reports, similar in nature to the report under investigation, may be sufficient to sustain an allegation of supervisorial neglect.

7. *Available Information May Suggest but Not Confirm That Abuse or Neglect Has Occurred.* Whether there is evidence to support an allegation may not be ascertainable without continuing the investigation and gathering detailed information from parents, children, and others who have pertinent data. Workers often request assistance from others, medical or psychological consultants for instance, before a final determination. For example, observations of a child's behavior may suggest internal injuries. This directs the worker to arrange for a medical examination. Or the child's behavior may seem so inappropriate as to suggest the need for a psychological evaluation. Should this occur, diagnostic assistance must be arranged. A final determination must await the diagnostic report.

protective custody, or emergency services sent into the home, if any of the dangerous conditions reviewed in the guidelines for an immediate home visit are found. Once it has been determined that credible evidence exists, whether from information supplied by a reporter or from evidence gathered by the worker during the first home visit, worker attention turns to problem assessment—to identifying the difficulties that must be resolved to ensure the child's safety. The process of conducting a problem assessment is described in the last half of this chapter.

Cases may be closed following a single home visit if supervision is adequate, the child well, and the home safe.

Types of Evidence

The information provided by a reporter, coupled with the information that a worker gathers during a visit to the family home, may be inconclusive, causing the case to be continued for further investigation. The course of the ongoing investigation will be governed by the nature of the report, the worker's observations, information elicited from family members and collateral resources, and information contained in agency archives. Before we discuss this process, let us look at the kinds of evidence staff may compile [1].

Real evidence consists of documents and photographs such as X-rays, pictures showing a child's injuries, certified school records showing patterns of attendance, and return receipts from letters sent by registered mail.

Direct evidence comes from firsthand knowledge of events. It takes the form of statements describing what an observer saw, heard, said, and did. The following narrative recorded by a protective service worker is illustrative:

> I arrived at the Mitchell home at 7:00 A.M. The front door was ajar. I heard a child crying from inside the apartment. I knocked on the door and called out, "Is anyone home?" but received no answer. I entered the apartment and found a young boy (Timothy, age 4) sitting in a corner of the living room. There was no adult in the home.

In some cases the only evidence available comes from lay reporters who observed a child being beaten or who overheard a caretaker threaten a youngster. Information elicited from reporters should be put in writing, using the informant's own words. Since facts may be distorted by time, information should be recorded at the earliest possible moment. Workers should try to have lay persons give depositions—testimony taken under oath—for use in court.

Hearsay evidence is secondhand information. The statement, "Mrs. Smith told me that she heard Mr. Williams threaten his son," is an example. Hearsay evidence is generally not admissible in court because its accuracy cannot be ascertained through cross-examination. If possible, the worker should try to obtain firsthand evidence from Mrs. Smith.

Figure 2.4 IS THERE CREDIBLE EVIDENCE OF ABUSE OR NEGLECT?

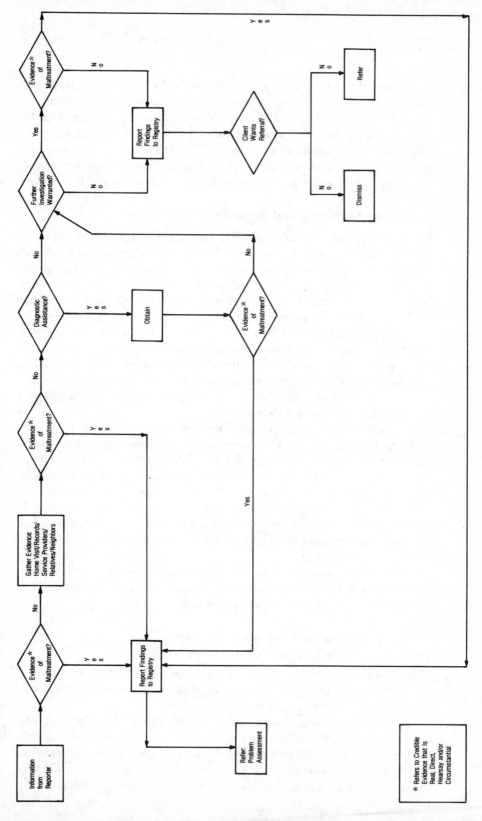

Circumstantial evidence is indirect proof of facts. For example, if medical opinion holds that a child's injuries could not have been sustained by accident and if we have knowledge of who was taking care of the child at the time the injury occurred, assuming that there was only one caretaker, we would infer that that person was responsible for the injuries. Circumstantial evidence plays a significant role in establishing the basis for action in protective service cases since direct proof of facts is often not available.

A Note on Gathering and Recording Information

Several references have been made to the use of information in court. All cases do not go to court, but the potential for court action is always present. (Guidelines for petitioning the court are presented on pages 58 through 59). Workers must know the kinds of evidence acceptable in court. It is incumbent on staff to search for such evidence. The court may dismiss a case if evidence is poorly documented—an action that may result in increased risk to a child. Whether or not the court is involved, protective service intervention reduces family privacy and diminishes parental control over children. This can be justified, however, when evidence shows that services are necessary to safeguard a child. Justification rests partly on gathering documentation, using guidelines such as those just reviewed, and includes the manner in which workers record information.

Workers should strive to record information in a descriptive manner, avoiding the use of labels and the temptation to draw inferences from observations. If a client says, "I am not sure whether I want to go for counseling," the client's statement should be recorded as a direct quotation. Inferential statements such as "The client is resistant to services," should not be used because they go beyond the facts. The client may be resistant to services. It is possible, however, that uncertainty about what to expect from counseling or previous experiences in which counseling was not productive may condition the response given.

Information contained in agency records and supplied by collateral resources often has limited usefulness for decision making because the information was recorded in an inferential manner.

Using Information to Determine Whether There Is Credible Evidence of Abuse or Neglect

Many, perhaps a majority, of the cases that come to the attention of protective services are "grey-area" cases in which there is no real or direct evidence of maltreatment or risk to a child.

Absent such evidence, workers must create a data base using their observations, information supplied by others, and that which is found in agency archives to formulate *risk hypotheses*. A risk hypothesis contains information describing the situation in which a child was found (whether the child was being supervised, for example), the condition of the child, or of the child's home. And it includes evidence suggestive of parental culpability, which is defined as an intention to cause harm and/or an unwillingness to take action to reduce imminent risk.

The information reported in risk hypotheses is one way of showing worker efforts to strike a balance between a child's right to be protected from injury and the right of parents to raise their children free of outside intervention. Evidence of parental culpability tips the scales in favor of the child and her right to be safeguarded from harm, hence justifying action by protective services.

The efforts workers undertake to create this balance should be clear from a review of the guidelines for determining whether a child is in immediate danger. Questions focusing on parental actions and intentions appear throughout. To illustrate this issue, consider the first section, which deals with supervision. Lack of supervision forms the basis for many of the reports made to protective services. Save for extreme cases, however, where a parent's inability to care for a child is beyond question or where an infant has been left unattended and a parent cannot be immediately located, determining what action to take is often difficult. Efforts to establish criteria for determining whether a child is safe that are based solely on the child's age, on the time of day the child is left alone, or the length of time the child is alone are arbitrary. This is why we focus attention on whether parents left instructions for their child, whether the child understands the instructions (e.g., knows what to do should she need help), and on whether the child is able to act on her own behalf.

We are not suggesting that parental decisions to leave children alone are necessarily correct decisions, but that it would be an error to infer neglect if the parent's decision rested on her assessment of her child's ability to care for herself. When one encounters situations in which parents acted according to their best judgment but in which, in the worker's judgment, the actions taken place a child at risk, the worker's major task is educational. Here, the basis for assuming risk is described to parents, and ways of reducing risk are explored, such as engaging a child care person, enrolling a youngster in day care, or teaching a child self-help skills. If a parent will not act to reduce risk, will not accept agency services, or if there are previous reports similar in nature to the report under investigation, a basis for protective service action can be established. Some examples of how workers document risk are as follows:

> John Smith, age 6, is left unsupervised each day between 2 P.M., when school ends, and 6 P.M., when his mother returns from work. There is neither a telephone in the home nor neighbors within walking distance to whom the child can turn for help. Mrs. Alicia Smith, mother, refuses to enroll John in day care, will not engage a child care person, and will not permit this worker to make arrangements for child care.

> Steven and Richard Hite, age 4 and 5 respectively, are left in the care of their elder sister, Michelle, age 14, each weekday evening from 7 P.M. until 2 A.M.

while their mother, Stephanie Hite, is at work. Michelle told this worker that she "sometimes goes out with friends," leaving the children to care for themselves. Mrs. Hite said that she sees "nothing wrong with this situation" and that she will not "spend good money on a babysitter."

Andrew Felix, father of Timothy and Jane Felix, twins, age 5, denies leaving his children unsupervised. There are two previous reports on the Felix family. Agency records show that Mr. Felix agreed to enroll his children in day care subsequent to the last report. Records of the Hillside Day Care Center show that Mr. Felix inquired into its program but did not follow up on his inquiry. Mr. Felix states that he chose to supervise his children himself rather than enroll them in day care. Since this is the third report it seems advisable to open this case to ensure that child care arrangements are made and followed through.

It is important to bear in mind that some of our concerns about a child's safety are generated more by differences between our own child rearing practices and those of others than they are by any evidence of imminent danger. Developing risk hypotheses according to the guidelines presented here is one way of reducing the chances that value judgments will exert an undue influence on decision making.

Some of the conditions that workers observe are caused by parents' lack of knowledge, skill, and income. A parent may not know what constitutes a well-balanced diet, may not know how to gain access to community resources when help is needed, may not know how to care for a newborn, or may be unable to afford child care services or home repairs. Here, too, it would not be reasonable to allege maltreatment unless the parent refused help when offered.

Certain types of allegations cannot be upheld without information from third parties. Whether or not a child is suffering from malnutrition is a medical determination. Charges of educational neglect generally require documentation from school authorities showing how often a child has been absent. Diagnostic assistance may be required because a worker has not been trained in certain assessment procedures. Several examples follow, showing how information from third parties is used to determine whether there is evidence to sustain charges of maltreatment.

Examples

Example 1

The Rodriguez family came to the attention of protective services following a report by a school social worker that Anita Rodriguez, age 14, had been truant from school several days each month for a 3-month period of time. School records showed that the school social worker had made seven attempts to reach Mrs. Rodriguez by telephone (none of the calls were returned) and had sent three letters to the mother describing Anita's truancy, asking Mrs. Rodriguez to contact the school to discuss Anita's absences. The letters were never answered. Two of the letters had been sent by registered mail, the return receipt indicating that the mother had received them.

Mrs. Rodriguez was no more cooperative with the protective service worker than she had been with the school social worker. Here, the key to supporting an allegation of educational neglect was the mother's tacit acceptance of her daughter's behavior, evidenced by her unwillingness to meet with school authorities. If Mrs. Rodriguez had been cooperative, this case would not have been opened to protective services on the basis of educational neglect. The mother's seeming lack of interest is required as evidence to support a petition of educational neglect. Without the documentation provided by the school social worker the charges would not have been upheld in court.

Example 2

A protective service worker observed bruises on a youngster's face and arms that the parent explained by saying that the child had fallen off her bicycle. The child confirmed the report. The worker arranged for the youngster to be examined by a physician, who subsequently reported that the location and type of injury could not have been sustained in the manner suggested. The conflict between the report of the parent and the physician is the key issue. The task that confronted the worker was to inform the parent of this conflict and to request a factual account of how the injuries were sustained.

The disparity between the report made by parent and child and that made by the physician is not proof of parental culpability. But unless a satisfactory explanation is offered, the lack of congruence would be a sufficient basis for hypothesizing that the parent caused the injury or was aware of who had caused it and was not willing to divulge this information.

In fact, the youngster's injuries were caused by the parent, who lost control while disciplining the child.

Example 3

During a home visit a worker observed a youngster sitting in a chair in a corner of a room. The child would not, when asked, sit by the worker and parent. Her response to questions was hesitant and her affect flat, i.e., her voice was monotonic and she did not look at the person to whom she was speaking.

The child's behavior could be caused by nervousness in the interview situation, indicate behavioral norms of a subculture different from that of the worker, or reflect a more generalized problem. To determine which hypothesis was correct, the worker sought information from different sources. He contacted the youngster's school, inquiring about her behavior in and outside of the classroom. He queried relatives and friends of the family and arranged to observe the child at school, at play, and interacting with the parents. He also arranged for psychological testing.

Additional information indicated that the behavior observed during the initial interview was consistent with the child's behavior elsewhere, and that they were not normative for her peer group. Thus, the suggestion that help was needed was a reasonable one.

The course of action that workers follow in situations such as this depends upon parental responses to the suggestion that help is necessary. If a parent accepts the suggestion that help is needed (and assuming that the parent has not previously withdrawn from a program designed to assist the family with this difficulty), services can be provided on a voluntary basis. The parent's willingness to accept assistance would not support a hypothesis that the parent's behavior was creating risk for the child. Whether service is offered by the protective agency or the client referred elsewhere would depend upon worker skill level, worker time to provide direct problem-solving services, and the availability of community programs to provide help.

If assistance is offered and refused, or if the client's service history raises doubts as to the likelihood of continuing with services on a voluntary basis, there would be sufficient grounds for proceeding on an involuntary basis. A refusal of help, in the face of evidence that it is needed, would support a hypothesis that the parent's concern for the youngster, as expressed in the refusal of help, is less than what is expected of parents in our society, thus falling below minimum standards.

There are situations in which a parent's behavior has not had an observable effect on a child but in which risk may exist. Parental expectations may be inappropriate to the child's age. For instance, a 3-year-old may be expected by her parent to eat all of the food on her plate, not to make a mess, and to pick up and put away all of her toys each time she finishes playing with them. The parent may report feeling extremely frustrated by the child's inability to live up to her expectations and may say that she cannot understand why her child is different from other 3-year-olds. When asked how she deals with her frustration, the client may say that she does not know what to do, but feels as though she might "explode."

The child cannot meet her parent's expectations due to her age. The parent's frustration level is high and her statement that she does not know how to deal with her feelings lends credibility to the suggestion that the child is in danger even though she has not been injured.

The child may never be injured. The point, however, is that the facts would lead a reasonable person to conclude that the possibility of risk exists and that intervention to reduce risk is warranted.

Risk hypotheses become less tenable as one moves away from the facts. An unreasonable hypothesis is usually replete with inferences and not supported by evidence. Often such hypotheses focus on long-range effects, such as the suggestion that a child whose parents are undergoing divorce will, ipso facto, suffer emotionally in the long run.

A Note on Risk Taking

Deciding whether to open a case to protective services or whether to leave children in the care of their parents involves an element of risk taking, since one cannot predict the course of events that will follow a home visit.

The only way to ensure a child's safety is to remove the youngster or to send a live-in caretaker into the home. Removing all of the children who are the subject of protective service reports, as a way of reducing risk, is a practical impossibility and one that would not be socially acceptable. Removal of children constitutes an extreme example of invasion of family privacy. Live-in caretakers may reduce risk temporarily, but eventually one must confront leaving children alone with their parents. There are no sure ways of eliminating risk. An example will illustrate the dilemma confronting workers.

Responding to a report of supervisorial neglect, the worker visited the Damien home, where the mother, Mrs. Damien, was present. She denied having left her 4-year-old son, William, unattended. The mother was a full-time homemaker who said that she either took her son with her when she left home or that she engaged a babysitter, whose name and telephone number she gave to the worker. The babysitter confirmed working for Mrs. Damien on occasion. There were no previous reports and no basis for further action. Twenty-four hours after the investigation, a fire broke out in the Damien home. William died of smoke inhalation. Mrs. Damien was not at home when the tragedy occurred.

Fortunately, a case such as this is exceptional. It does, however, illustrate a dilemma of protective service work. The dilemma is that workers are interested in processes or patterns of child care that occur over time but process information is difficult to obtain and is rarely available when initial decisions with critical implications for a child's safety have to be made. Patterns of child care may be established if previous reports exist or if services were provided and client behavior rigorously documented, and, as we shall see in the last half of this chapter, information descriptive of processes can be gathered during case assessment.

The facts gathered by the worker in the Damien case would not have supported any course of action other than the one taken by the worker. Clearly, Mrs. Damien's behavior 24 hours after the visit could not have been predicted.

When there is neither evidence of abuse or neglect nor a basis for inferring risk, clients are referred for services if they want assistance with problems that fall outside of the purview of protective services. The facts gathered during the investigation are reported to the state central registry.

The form shown in figure 2.5 is used to indicate whether there is evidence of abuse or neglect. If there is, workers indicate the type(s) of neglect and/or abuse found by placing a check in the column to the right of the list of allegations. The type(s) of evidence that supports the allegations is indicated

Figure 2.5 **IS THERE CREDIBLE EVIDENCE THAT ABUSE OR NEGLECT HAD OCCURRED OR THAT THE CHILD IS AT RISK OF EITHER?**

YES _____ NO _____ UNCERTAIN AT THIS TIME _____

If YES, please indicate the specific allegation and source of evidence on the following checklist.

Allegation	Check as many as apply	SOURCE AND TYPE OF EVIDENCE [a] (Insert number code for type of evid. in column indicating source)								Is Evidence [d]	
		DCFS Worker	Med.	Collateral Psych.	Collateral Other	Lay Report	Parent	Child	Other (specify)	Direct	Hypo.
*Death											
*Physical abuse [b] severe ___ moderate ___ mild ___											
*Sexual abuse											
Sexual molestation											
Sexual exploitation											
**Emotional abuse											
Abandonment											
Lack of supervision											
*Medical neglect [c]											
*Malnutrition											

YES _____ NO _____ UNCERTAIN AT THIS TIME _____

If YES, please indicate the specific allegation and source of evidence on the following checklist.

Allegation	Check as many as apply	SOURCE AND TYPE OF EVIDENCE [a] (Insert number code for type of evid. in column indicating source)								Is Evidence [d]	
		DCFS Worker	Med.	Collateral Psych.	Collateral Other	Lay Report	Parent	Child	Other (specify)	Direct	Hypo.
Shelter neglect											
Clothing neglect											
***Educational neglect											

*Require medical evidence.

**Requires psychological evaluation.

***Must be substantiated by school records.

[a] *Types of Evidence:*

(1) X-rays (2) photos (3) med. exam (4) psych. test (5) written report from collateral (6) worker observ. in home (7) worker observ. in office (8) school records (9) taped interview (10) client self-report (11) signed deposition (12) case record (13) registry information (14) court report (15) other.

[b] Includes poisoning if medical evidence suggests intent, and drug/alcohol use if there is evidence that parent encouraged use. Poisoning due to a child's ingesting drugs that were not properly stored should be categorized as inadequate supervision.

[c] Physical conditions that require medical attention and the parent will not use resources voluntarily. Also includes failure to thrive.

[d] Direct = parent acknowledges act; reporter observed child being beaten. Hypothetical = reasonable cause to open case, no direct evidence.

(for example, X-rays or worker observations) by inserting a code number in the column under the heading that identifies the source of information. Whether evidence is direct or hypothetical is noted in the far righthand column.

IS IT NECESSARY TO PETITION THE COURT?

State law or agency policy may require workers to petition the juvenile court to assume jurisdiction over children under certain sets of circumstances. A petition may be necessary whenever there is evidence of abuse or neglect or any time a child is placed out of the home.

Absent statutory or policy requirements, the decision whether to file a court petition is generally left to worker and supervisory discretion. If parents will not cooperate with protective services, if there is reason to question whether parents who agree to work cooperatively will do so (for example, if agency records show that the parents have not been cooperative in the past), or if clients withdraw from services and there is reason to think that withdrawal creates risk for a child, a decision to petition the court may be made (see fig. 2.6). The question whether one should file a petition with the court may arise more than once in the course of providing services.

Professional opinion differs on the subject of court involvement. One position holds that involving the court increases the likelihood that parents will cooperate with service providers. It is assumed that the authority of the court will be instrumental in keeping parents involved. Contrary to this is the suggestion that invoking court action impedes the development of a positive working relationship between worker and client, since it emphasizes the law enforcement aspects of a worker's role. This latter position questions the basis for filing a court petition when parents agree to work cooperatively.

The debate whether to involve the court all of the time or only when parents are not cooperative remains open. Until we have data from controlled studies showing level of parental involvement with service providers as a function of whether the court is involved, the issue will remain unsettled.

Figure 2.6 IS IT NECESSARY TO PETITION THE COURT?

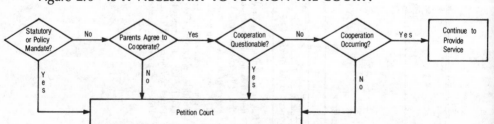

Assuming that the decision is left to the discretion of staff, we recommend that the court should be petitioned only if:

1. There is credible evidence of abuse or neglect and the parents are not willing to cooperate with protective services;
2. Protective services were offered on a voluntary basis and records show that parents withdrew from services against a worker's advice;
3. A child is in placement and parents are not cooperating with a plan to move the child into a permanent home;
4. Parents withdraw from a voluntary service program and there is evidence that this places the child in danger.

IS OUT-OF-HOME PLACEMENT NECESSARY?

Deciding whether to place a child in out-of-home care is, with few exceptions, one of the most difficult choices that child welfare staff members face. The overriding importance of maintaining children in their own homes is reflected in federal law, the statutes and policies of many state agencies, and the writings of social work professionals. Before reviewing conditions that warrant placement away from the home, reasons for taking a conservative stand on this subject are noted.

Recognizing that placement in foster care can provide temporary relief for families during periods of crisis and that such relief may be important to stabilize family life, it must also be recognized that placement can exacerbate family difficulties. Separating a child from her parents can be traumatic for the youngster, who may blame herself for the separation. Parents can be made to feel inadequate, or their feelings for their children may become attenuated. This may cause parents to withdraw from ongoing contact with their children, foreclosing the possibility that children will be reunited with them.

When parents have been receiving AFDC, they may lose some or all of their grant following placement of a child. Unless parents are able to replace lost income through employment, they may be forced to relocate. If new accommodations are not adequate to house their children, they may be forced to again relocate before their children are returned to their care. Unless parents have money or resources, finding adequate housing may be impossible without restoration of their AFDC grant.

Resolving problems that necessitated placement can prove difficult once children enter care. Assessment and intervention frequently occur under artificial conditions—in the foster home or worker's office, for example—rather than in the family's natural environment, which offers the optimal framework for identifying problems and effecting behavior change.

Therefore, every effort should be made to provide services to children in their own homes. If services are not available or if the evidence suggests that risk to a child cannot be reduced through provision of at-home services, efforts should be made to place children with relatives or family friends who can be licensed as foster parents in order to maintain continuity in the child's relationships (see fig. 2.7). Out-of-home placement is appropriate if:

1. There is no adult willing to care for a child, or the child refuses to stay in the home.
2. There is medical evidence that physical abuse or nutritional neglect is so severe as to be life-threatening.
3. There was intent to kill the child, even if injury is not severe. Medical evidence should support a hypothesis of deliberate poisoning, or marks on the child's body should indicate assault with a deadly weapon or repeated beating with a heavy object.
4. There is medical or psychological evidence of abuse or neglect that, without intervention, may threaten the child's life, *and* the parent refuses help.
5. Medical evidence of repeated abuse exists. This reference is to previous untreated injuries, generally identified through X-rays, where the location or type of injury suggests prior maltreatment.
6. Severe abuse or neglect recurs after services were offered.

Figure 2.7   IS OUT-OF-HOME PLACEMENT NECESSARY?

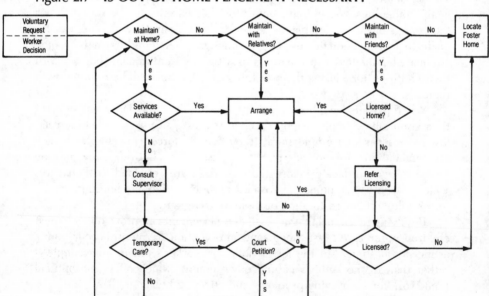

turbance or withdrawal by the child, *and* the parent rejects the child.

8. Medical or psychological evidence suggests that the parent is incompetent to provide minimum child care and there are no resources (e.g., family, friends, or community services) to help in the home while assessment is under way.

9. A child has been raped by a related adult or a nonrelated adult known to the parent, *and* the parent did not attempt to protect the child.

WHAT IS THE MOST APPROPRIATE PLACEMENT FACILITY?

The choice of a placement facility should be made in the context of long-range case objectives and should be governed by knowledge of the conditions most likely to facilitate family reunification, since, in the great majority of cases, placement will be short-term, with the objective of reuniting children with their parents (see fig. 2.8).

Figure 2.8 **WHAT IS THE MOST APPROPRIATE PLACEMENT FACILITY?**

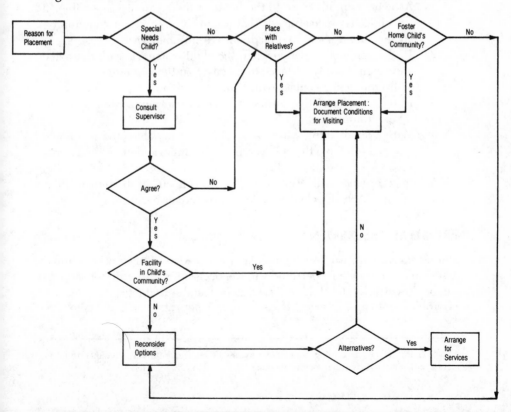

The probabilities of achieving family reunification are greatest during a child's first year to 18 months in placement. The likelihood of realizing this outcome decreases thereafter. Parental visiting of children in care is critical to achieving restoration. Thus, selection of an initial placement must maximize the chances for early and frequent visits between children and their parents.

Parental visits are partly a function of the geographic proximity of the foster home to the residence of parents because many families cannot afford costly transportation and, especially in some rural areas, public transportation may not be available. Moreover, the frequency of visits may decrease as the length of time the parent must spend traveling increases. Finally, continual contact between parents and children should not be contingent upon the availability of agency personnel to provide transportation.

Placement decisions should not be governed solely by the child's needs unless the parent is incarcerated or hospitalized and will not be released for 18 months or more, or the child has special treatment needs that require placement in a treatment facility, or there is evidence that the parent has abandoned the youngster.

In sum, children should be placed:

1. As geographically close to the home of their parents as possible. If the child has special needs that cannot be met in her community, arrangements should be made for parent-child visits.
2. In the home of a relative when the child is familiar with the home and when there is evidence to suggest that the youngster will benefit from ongoing contact with family members.
3. In the least restrictive setting that most closely approximates a family environment.
4. With a family of the same race, whenever possible, and in a home that will reinforce the child's religious, ethnic, and/or cultural heritage.
5. In accordance with criteria set forth in rule 307 of the Indian Child Welfare Act, if a child is of American Indian heritage.

PROBLEM ASSESSMENT

During assessment, workers identify family problems in need of resolution. Assessment information contributes to the decision whether or not services will be provided by the child welfare agency,* and it facilitates the selection of problem-solving strategies. If assessment is not rigorous, dangers to chil-

---

*Agency policy, describing populations to be served and outlining eligibility requirements, and state law are other factors affecting this decision.

dren may increase because the problems creating the greatest risks may be overlooked. Clients may receive inappropriate services, since those chosen rest on information compiled by workers during this phase. Conversely, failure to identify family strengths may result in providing services unnecessarily.

The procedures described in this section apply to both protective and voluntary programs. Guidelines for selecting assessment strategies and determining whether cases should be served by the child welfare agency are presented.

The Purpose of Assessment: An Overview

In chapter one, in the context of discussing the general nature of presenting problems, it was said that the information workers need to decide whether to open a case can be described at three levels. The first is the labels clients use to describe their problems; the second, examples of the behaviors, thoughts, and feelings to which the client is referring by use of general labels; and examples of the situations in which problems occur, including identification of significant others involved in the problem. Information descriptive of behaviors, thoughts, feelings, and situations gives direction to an in-depth assessment by highlighting the behavioral, cognitive, and affective components of a problem, and by focusing attention on the situational contexts in which assessment should occur. This sets the stage for gathering the third level of information describing the specific circumstances in which problems occur, as well as the frequency or severity of the problem. These data enable the worker to identify the specific conditions to be modified and provide a basis for measuring progress in problem resolution during service provision. To illustrate the importance of this information, consider the following.

Allegations are the charges made against parents that serve to justify opening a case to protective services. Evidence collected during the investigation is used to support allegations in ways previously reviewed. The categories we use to explain why cases are opened, e.g., physical or sexual abuse, supervisorial neglect, and so forth, do not provide sufficient information for identifying problem-solving strategies, since any of these problems may be caused by different factors. What professionals label as supervisorial neglect, for instance, may be the result of parental beliefs regarding the age at which a child should be taught self-help skills; or it may be due to income deficiencies that preclude paying for day care services; or to a lack of knowledge of how to gain access to community day care programs; or it may be the result of neglect, which is defined as parental indifference to whether a child is being supervised.

Parental beliefs about teaching a child self-help skills, income deficiencies, lack of knowledge of how to gain access to day care programs, or indifference to supervision are different *antecedent* conditions that can result in the same problem. Also, parental behaviors may be maintained by positive outcomes. For instance, a child may be acquiring and demonstrating self-help skills, and the parent may find the free time she gains by leaving her child alone to be a rewarding outcome. If a child has not been injured when left by herself, the parent is reinforced in her thinking that it is appropriate to leave the child alone.

Some parents dislike leaving a child unsupervised. A single, working parent may be uncomfortable at the thought that her child is alone between the end of the school day and the time that the parent returns from work. However, the options of giving up her job to stay at home or paying for child care can reduce her net income below what she would receive from an AFDC grant and could be more distasteful than leaving the youngster by herself. Problem-solving strategies will differ depending upon the circumstances that gave rise to and maintain problems.

Although the previous example is taken from protective services, staff members in voluntary programs also seek to uncover antecedent and maintaining conditions. The chief difference between these service areas, with regard to assessment procedures, is that workers in protective services use allegations as a starting point for assessment whereas those in voluntary programs use problems identified by clients or referring sources.

Antecedent conditions are sometimes identified before formal assessment begins.* Information gathered during an investigation or the first contact with clients who have requested voluntary services can point to problems whose resolution should be undertaken immediately; or information provided by collaterals who have conducted a thorough assessment before referring a case may lead to decisions to implement certain services at once.

For example, a psychological consultant has diagnostic information that shows that a parent's knowledge and/or skills in certain areas of child care are deficient. The consultant hypothesizes that the deficiencies identified were instrumental to an abusive or neglectful act. Recommendations for intervention in the form of parent education classes and the use of teaching homemakers or public health nurses to provide parent training might follow. Substitute care services may be offered to a single parent who must be hospitalized for a brief period of time and does not have family or friends who can assist with child care. A client's need for medical care, or income deficiencies that prevent the client from obtaining food or from making home repairs, may be readily apparent to a worker who recommends that certain

---

*Data useful for assessment purposes may be gathered during an investigation or during the first contact with clients requesting voluntary services. Formal assessment refers to that phase of intake in which purposeful decisions are made as to how, where, and by whom detailed data descriptive of client problems will be acquired.

types of assistance be provided immediately. Skills deficits, the need to enter the hospital, and income deficiencies are examples of antecedent conditions that must be identified if correct problem-solving strategies are to be chosen.

BEGINNING ASSESSMENT

The process that workers follow to identify antecedent and maintaining conditions in order to specify problems in need of resolution is shown in figure 2.9. The information recorded on the problem profile gives direction to the assessment process. As noted above, the behaviors that define client problems provide a focus for initial observations. The situations listed indicate the context in which observation is most likely to be fruitful and includes places where problem behaviors are displayed, as well as people whose presence elicits and/or maintains problematic behaviors. Protective service staff complete a problem profile using information gathered during the investigation. Workers in both program areas add information to the profile when they first meet with all family members and when or if new problems are identified at subsequent meetings. The information that protective service workers record on the profile differs in certain ways from that recorded by staff in voluntary services. Before describing these differences, some comments regarding information culled from agency records and other service providers are in order.

Information From Records and Service Providers

The use of information from agency records and persons who have provided services to clients has been noted at several points in the preceding material. We have seen that previous reports of maltreatment and information provided by reporters can contribute to determining whether there is credible evidence of abuse or neglect. The chance that collateral resources may have diagnostic information was also noted. If collaterals have diagnostic or assessment information that is directly related to problems of current concern, child welfare staff members can avoid duplication of assessment tasks. For example, a public health nurse may have been working with a family on whom an abuse report was subsequently filed. The nurse might have detailed information regarding a parent's child-care skills, including identification of deficits that were considered possible antecedents to the act of maltreatment. It would be wasteful of resources for a worker to undertake or arrange for an assessment and duplicate tasks already completed. Knowledge of services currently being provided and information regarding the efficacy of previous services can enable the selection of intervention strategies. Problem-solving approaches that were not effective with a family can be

Figure 2.9 **WHAT ARE THE SPECIFIC PROBLEMS IN NEED OF RESOLUTION?**

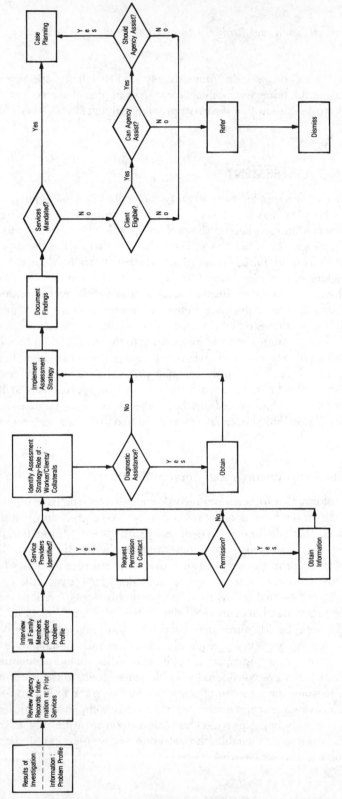

eliminated from consideration. Effective approaches can be tried again.

Guidelines for determining the usefulness of information available in case records and from collaterals are presented later when procedures for selecting assessment strategies are reviewed.

When assessment first begins, one need record only such general information as the type of service received, problems addressed, and the identity of the provider. Such information may be recorded before the first home visit (see fig. 2.10). Additional information will be elicited from family members whose permission to contact collaterals for detailed data is requested. Out of respect for client confidentiality, contact is made only with a client's permission and only if there is reason to think that a resource person has information pertinent to the issues being addressed.

Clients should be told how information provided by others will be used for their benefit, for instance, by eliminating the need to subject family members to repetitive assessment procedures and to facilitate the selection of appropriate service strategies. But information provided by others can be used against clients should a case go to court; that information can be used this way must be shared with the client as well.

Protective Service Problem Profile

Protective services workers begin to develop the problem profile during the investigation. The problem profile shown in figure 2.11 differs from the one presented in chapter 1 in the information recorded in column 2, where the allegation(s) is listed; column 3, where suspected antecedent conditions are reported; column 4, where the source of identification of antecedents is noted; and column 5, in which examples of antecedents are listed. The information recorded in the column headed "Problems Identified by Family Members" is analogous to the column headed "Label" in our prior example. The remaining items of information are the same.

INTERVIEWING ALL FAMILY MEMBERS: A FRAMEWORK FOR GATHERING INITIAL ASSESSMENT INFORMATION

Assessment strategies, including specification of the role to be played by the worker, family members, and collateral resources, must be discussed. To identify strategies, the worker meets with all members of the family in their home. Generally, two meetings are sufficient for this purpose. A framework outlining items of information the worker seeks to gather during these meetings is presented next.

The perceptions of all family members regarding the problems listed on the profile, or the explanations offered regarding the circumstances surrounding an incident of maltreatment, are elicited first.

Figure 2.10 INFORMATION REGARDING USE OF SERVICES

PART I (1) Is the client/family currently receiving services from the agency?   Yes ____ No ____

  (2) If NO, has the client/family received services within the last 2 years?   Yes ____ No ____

  (a) If YES to 1 or 2, complete the following, then go to Part II.
  If NO to 1 and 2, go directly to Part II.

Service	Use		If past, date closed	Name of		Name of service recipient if different from family name
	current	past		worker	supervisor	
1. financial (insert type in 2, e.g., AFDC, general assistance)						
2. _____						
3. food stamps						
4. Medicare						
5. Medicaid						
6. day care						
7. homemaker						
8. protective service						
9. foster care						
10. adoption						
11. other (insert type) _____ _____						

PART II (1) Is the client/family receiving services from another community agency?   Yes ____ No ____

(2) If NO, has the client/family received services within the last 2 years?   Yes ____ No ____

    (a) If YES to 1 or 2, complete the following and request permission to contact the resource to learn about the services provided.

    (b) If NO to 1 and 2, do not complete this form.

Agencies	Service dates		Name of counselor/ worker	Problems addressed	Services provided
	from	to			
1. Name _____ Address _____ Telephone _____					
2. Name _____ Address _____ Telephone _____					
3. Name _____ Address _____ Telephone _____					

Figure 2.11   **PROBLEM PROFILE**

Problem Number	Allegation	Suspected Antecedents	Who Identified Antecedents	Examples of Antecedents	Problems Identified by Family
1	physical abuse	1. parent's expectations of child: inappropriate 2. uses physical discipline only	Ms. Young: public health Mr. Hillegos: protective service worker	1. mother expects child (age 4) to stay neat & clean at all times, including when she plays outside 2. mother expects child to pick up her toys & put them away immediately after playing with them 3. mother expects child to make her own bed immediately each day & to keep her room neat	

The worker shares the problem profile with all family members. He gathers information from those persons who were not present when the profile was first developed by posing a series of questions to learn whether members of the family perceive the problems listed on the profile as problems, whether the behavioral and situational examples offered match those listed, whether there are additional problems of concern, and whether there are strengths that have been overlooked.

Information provided by family members can add perspective to problems that may be missing when information comes from a single person. For example, the fact that family members disagree about problems is important information. Disagreement may prevent parents and children from having fruitful discussions of issues that one person considers problematic, where lack of discussion itself contributes to the perception of an issue as troublesome.

If a profile has not been completed, it is begun at this time. In the case of voluntary requests for service, workers ask family members to identify the problems necessitating the request. Protective service staff members start an interview by asking for information regarding the circumstances that sur-

Behavioral Examples If Different From Antecedents	Who Has the Problem Identified by Family	Date	Situational Context for Problems Identified by Family	Family Assets
		5/20		1. mother shows affection to child (hugs and kisses her, plays with her)
				2. child is obedient to the best of her ability

round an incident or a series of incidents of maltreatment. The request, "Please describe what you and your son were doing, what you were thinking about or feeling just before Johnny was injured," is illustrative.

Information regarding the history of the problem and about services used in relation to the problem is elicited next.

The worker asks whether a problem is of recent origin or whether it is a long-standing one. Whether it was triggered by an identifiable event is also determined. For instance, did the birth of a child, loss of employment, separation from a mate, or a death in the family precipitate a crisis? Or did a recent crisis force the family to deal with a long-standing problem that had been ignored? Knowing whether a problem was precipitated by a crisis or is the result of a characteristic set of behaviors can aid in the selection of appropriate problem-solving strategies.

As already noted, knowledge of the kind and efficacy of services offered in the past for similar problems contributes to decision making. The worker inquires into the family's service history and records information provided on the form presented in figure 2.10.

Family Interaction

The worker may observe patterns of interaction that hint at problematic family dynamics. For instance, a parent who has requested services may describe her son as unmanageable. Behavioral examples offered might include the child's unwillingness to listen to his mother and to follow her instructions. During an interview, the worker may observe that the parent interrupts the youngster each time he tries to contribute information.

The parent, by repeatedly interrupting her son, is modeling the behavior she finds distasteful. The worker hypothesizes that the boy's not listening is partly a result of following a parental example.

A child's behavior may be provocative. A young boy may "sass" a parent and imply by his manner of speaking that he does not respect his mother. Such observations and the inferences drawn from them are suggestive, not conclusive; they are best viewed as providing direction for further assessment.

Additional family assets are identified, such as positive feelings family members display toward each other, respect shown through attentive listening behavior, and parenting skills that are demonstrated. Information regarding significant others—relative and friends, for example—who might help the parent is also sought. The client's personal and environmental strengths should be capitalized on during the problem-solving phase.

Changes that family members would like to see come about through participation in service delivery programs are identified. Here, one is concerned with whether expectations are realistic. Does a parent expect that, as a result of receiving counseling services, her 15-year-old will obey instructions at all times, without argument? Expectations reported by parents can reveal potential problems. For instance, unrealistic expectations of a very young child may, when not met, result in an abusive act. Finally, direction for selecting intervention strategies can be gleaned from stated expectations. For example, a parent who reports that she is depressed may, when asked what she expects from services (or what she would be doing if she were not depressed), report that she would like to be spending more of her time with other adults. Identification of desired changes is likely to identify problem-solving objectives, and help the worker and client keep a positive focus on their work together.

Information acquired in the areas reviewed above may be recorded in a narrative format. Hypotheses regarding conditions that contribute to the onset of a problem—instructions to oneself, for example, to contact service providers identified by family members, and comments and impressions formed during the interview—can be recorded on a client interview memo (fig. 2.12). Recordings should be made immediately following the interview, before facts are lost to memory and events modified by impressions.

Figure 2.12   **CLIENT INTERVIEW MEMO**

Memo No. _____ Date _____ Time of Recording ____
Time of Interview _____ Person(s) Contacted _____
Method of Contact: in person _____ phone _____ mail _____

WORKER'S HYPOTHESES

Problem No. and Label from Profile	Behavior Observed	Hypotheses Regarding Controlling Conditions	Data Source	Date
1. Son is unmanageable	Mother interrupts son each time he tries to contribute information	1. Mother is modeling distasteful behavior 2. Son may be following parental example.	Worker	

SERVICE PROVIDERS TO BE CONTACTED AND PURPOSE OF CONTACT

COMMENTS AND WORKER IMPRESSIONS
Arrange observations of mother/son dialogue to see if behavior described above is typical of verbal interaction. If so, problem resolution may rest on teaching more appropriate methods of verbal interaction.

EVALUATING ASSESSMENT STRATEGIES

Client self-reports (which include interviews, inventories, and self-monitoring); direct observation by trained staff; information stored in agency records and that which is provided by collateral resources who have worked with, or are currently working with clients; are the main sources of assessment data. Each source has its strengths and weaknesses, an understanding of which can help in the selection of appropriate strategies for assessment [3:99–135].

Client Self-Reports

Information is gathered directly from clients by interviews, testing, and client self-monitoring. The *interview* is one of the easiest methods of gathering data. Its main requirement is that staff talk to clients to gain information. The main advantages of the interview, in addition to the fact that it is easy to use, is that clients can be questioned about past behavior and future expectations, and information regarding private thoughts, feelings, and behaviors, can be gained. Information provided during interviews, however, may not be accurate. The desire to look good, even though one is asking for help; embarrassment at revealing personal information; the fallibility of memory and the modification of events by subsequent thoughts, feelings, and impressions; may distort information. Finally, most of us do not observe our own behavior in detail, hence information provided is likely to be general rather than specific.

Inventories such as the Minnesota Multiphasic Personality Inventory or the California Personality Inventory* can be administered by psychologists in an effort to learn about client traits. Trait theories assume that people "react to many different stimuli with the same sort of responses" [8:537]. The usefulness of information provided by personality testing is a function of whether people do, indeed, respond in consistent ways. If they do, it should be possible to predict behavior in nontest situations. However, if behavior varies in relation to different stimuli, places, and people, predictability is limited. In fact, correlations between responses to paper-and-pencil test and nontest behavior are generally weak [9:77,79]. Thus, while personality tests are easily administered, their usefulness for contributing to assessment is limited.

Clients may be asked to report on their own behavior by responding to *checklists*. A checklist contains a series of items designed to elicit information in selected areas. A client may be asked to rate a child on each checklist item by indicating, for example, whether the youngster completes household chores or returns home on time, some of the time, all of the time, rarely, or never. Checklists are easy to use. They are especially useful when clients cannot clearly state their reasons for labeling their child "unmanageable or uncooperative."

Short-form scales, such as those developed by Walter Hudson and his associates, can be completed by the client and scored by the worker in only a few minutes. They can aid in problem specification as well as be administered repeatedly for continual feedback regarding problem change. Some

---

*These tests are considered objective because the subject is asked to respond directly to questions by agreeing or disagreeing with statements such as "I never think of unusual sexual situations." This is in contrast to subjective tests, such as the Thematic Apperception Test or the Rorschach, in which subjects are asked to free associate by describing what they see in an inkblot or other ambiguous pictures. The assumption underlying the latter tests is that people project themselves into the situations depicted and that their thoughts can be interpreted according to psychoanalytic theory (8:537–542). In reality, the results of subjective tests may say more about the theoretical orientation of the tester than the problems of the client.

scales that are available include *Parental Attitudes Towards Children, Child's Attitude Towards Mother, Child's Attitude Towards Father, The Index of Self-Esteem,* and *Generalized Contentment Scale* [6]. The accuracy of information reported in checklists and short-form scales can be affected by some of the same issues covered in the discussion of interviews.

Workers frequently want detailed information descriptive of client behaviors, thoughts, or feelings at the time they arise, as well as information about the situations and persons in whose presence the behaviors, thoughts, or feelings are elicited. This technique is called *self-monitoring.* Accuracy can be increased if information is recorded at the time the behaviors are displayed or the thoughts held. Clients can be asked to record information in journals or diaries. Tape recordings and checklists are additional ways in which clients report on their behavior.

If clients are trained in self-observation and recording, the likelihood of obtaining detailed information increases. The fact that clients are present when problems occur and that they can describe private thoughts, feelings, and behaviors, hence providing information regarding processes that workers may not have access to, is a distinct advantage of client self-recording.

Direct Observation by Professionals

Child welfare workers and professionals in other disciplines gather assessment data through direct observation of clients in an office setting or in the client's natural environment. Data may be gathered during simulations or from observations under naturalistic conditions.

Using simulations, workers create situations and ask clients to act out certain behaviors. Assume that a father refers to his child as unmanageable. Behavioral examples listed on the problem profile may center on verbal communication—for instance, "My son and I can't talk about anything without fighting" or "My son never listens to what I say." In structuring a simulation, the worker would ask father and son to select a topic of concern to them, and to discuss the topic for a set period of time. The worker could tape record the conversation or, using predeveloped coding forms [4:198–231], could record his observations of parent-child interaction: "Information can be gathered on who dominates the conversation, whether each gives the other the opportunity to talk, how responsive the listener is to the speaker, and so forth" [12:125].

Workers can also engage in direct observation in the client's natural environment. If the problem behaviors are said to occur during mealtime (the "Situations" column on the profile gives this information), the worker would elect to visit the home and observe at that time. Observation may occur in any setting where the behaviors of concern are most likely to be displayed.

The main weakness of simulations is that they are carried out under artificial conditions. Thus, the behaviors displayed may not indicate what transpires under natural conditions. This difficulty can be overcome by using other data-gathering methods, such as client self-reports. Information gathered in different ways is compared for consistency. Inconsistencies can be resolved by gathering additional assessment information.

On the plus side, observations during simulations are easier to set up. The range of behaviors can be restricted, and distracting stimuli can be reduced or eliminated. Observation under natural conditions is not as easy, given the variety of behaviors that may be displayed, the fact that competing stimuli cannot be easily controlled, and the time requirements in visiting clients at home.

The accuracy of information obtained is a function of the training a worker receives in direct observation and recording, the availability of recording forms that preclude the necessity of making detailed notes, and the careful selection of the behaviors to be observed and recorded, since there are limits to the number of observations that can be made and recorded. If workers tape conversations, they must learn how to analyze the contents of tapes.

Data gathered through observations during simulations and under natural conditions are a valuable source of assessment information. Acquiring information on problem behaviors when they are displayed can yield detailed data not accessible through interviews and client self-recording.

Collateral Resources

The use of information acquired from collateral resources has been mentioned previously. Since collaterals may use any of the data-gathering methods just reviewed, the usefulness of the information they have can be determined by applying the guidelines described above.

Information in Case Records, Court Reports, and Central Registries

Whether information from these sources can contribute to assessment depends upon the following: "where information is stored, the requirements for access and the volume of information contained in records. Privacy and confidentiality requirements may limit access. Further, records are often unorganized and written in vague language making it difficult to find specific items" [12:126].

Data from these sources is best viewed as directing attention to areas in which additional information should be acquired.

IDENTIFYING ASSESSMENT STRATEGIES

As the review above makes clear, each of the assessment strategies available to workers has its strengths and weaknesses. Strategies selected can differ as a function of the problem to be addressed. For example, when there are difficulties in parent-child interaction, direct observation of clients is called for. However, if a client is depressed to the extent that she is neglecting her children, client self-reports of the private thoughts, behaviors, and feelings that define depression are appropriate. Since strategies selected will differ in relation to the problem at hand, we must begin by reviewing how problems are given priorities and selected for in-depth assessment.

Problem Selection

Direction for problem assessment is found in an agency's service mandate, which is articulated in policy or state law. If an agency defines as its mission the provision of assistance to all families for whatever problems they present, the topic of problem selection is irrelevant. A more narrow statement of purpose, such as the provision of assistance only with those problems affecting a child's well-being, restricts the range of issues that concern workers. The relationship of policy to problem selection is discussed later in detail when guidelines for deciding whether to open a case to the agency are presented.

Regardless of which position an agency takes, problems must be given an order of priority. Efforts to intervene simultaneously on a host of difficulties would be overwhelming when problem resolution requires ongoing, active participation by clients.* The guidelines that follow presume that the goal of service provision is to maintain children in their own homes, or to reunite those in foster care with their families, as first priority. Moreover, it is assumed that problems selected will be those for which there is evidence to suggest that without agency intervention children are at risk in the present or near future.

1. Priority is given to problems that create risk for children, where risk is defined to include possible maltreatment, danger where there is no imputation of parental fault, and separation from the child's family of origin. In some instances, whether or not a problem is creating

---

*Resolution of some problems, those requiring financial, medical, or housing assistance, for example, may involve a set of relatively simple client tasks (completing forms for determination of eligibility, for instance) in contrast to those problems whose resolution requires that clients go to counseling on a weekly basis and undertake a series of "homework" assignments.

risk can be determined from information recorded on the profile and narrative and/or assessment data supplied by collateral resources. In other instances, a period of continuing assessment is necessary to reach a determination.

In the former category are difficulties whose resolution is found in providing assistance with financial, medical, housing, and food, and problems in which antecedent conditions, such as deficiencies in child care skills, have been identified. This was illustrated at the beginning of this section where the use of diagnostic information provided by consultants was briefly discussed.

2. Action to assist clients with certain problems cannot be undertaken until other difficulties are resolved. If a client has an incapacitating drug or alcohol problem and deficits in child care skills, the former will require attention before the latter can be dealt with.*

3. The court may establish certain conditions for leaving a child at home or as contingencies for family reunification, such as ordering client involvement in a counseling program. A worker may disagree with a judicial decision, but unless he is able to have a judge rescind an order, the stipulation will have to be addressed.

4. Resource deficits can force priorities. A worker's best judgment may be that parent training should receive preference over counseling for personal problems. If space in a training program is not available and assuming that alternative methods of training do not exist, implementing this service may have to be deferred.**

To the extent possible, priorities should be negotiated with clients. This is an easier task in voluntary than in protective programs. In the latter, client choice to participate may be more illusory than real, since the client often knows that nonparticipation can result in negative sanctions being levied, such as the filing of criminal charges or removal of a child.

When services are voluntary and when the worker's decision regarding priorities differs from the client's, the worker explains the reasoning for his position, focusing on the presumed risks to a child if problems go unresolved. Clients can elect not to use agency services if the issues they want addressed do not receive priority.

GENERAL GUIDELINES FOR SELECTING ASSESSMENT STRATEGIES

To summarize, selection of assessment strategies begins with an overview of family problems that is recorded on the problem profile. This is

---

*The assumption here is that deficits in child care skills and a substance abuse problem are not such as to necessitate removal of a child.
**An unfortunate consequence of resource deficits is that children may have to be removed, temporarily, until services can be offered.

supplemented by information provided by collaterals and that which is gathered during an initial home visit or visits with the family, recorded in narrative form. Before assessment strategies are selected, problems are given priorities by using the suggestions just reviewed.

Once problems have been given priorities, decide whether assistance is required with assessment. For example, are there problems that are clearly medical or legal in nature? Is it necessary to determine whether clients are eligible for financial, medical, or housing assistance? If assistance is required, request help.

Next, determine whether agency policy requires certain types of assessment data. For instance, policy may require psychological testing of a child if the child's special needs are the basis for a voluntary request for out-of-home placement. Again, request assistance when necessary.

When workers assume responsibility for conducting an assessment, they use information from family members and collaterals to formulate initial hypotheses regarding the antecedent and maintaining conditions for the problem to be addressed.

FORMULATING AND USING HYPOTHESES TO GUIDE SELECTION OF ASSESSMENT STRATEGIES

We have said that workers use information from three sources to formulate hypotheses about antecedent and maintaining conditions. These sources are (1) the problem profile, (2) the narrative that is completed following home visits with all family members, and (3) information provided by collaterals.

Now, in the context of case examples, we will review the process of formulating hypotheses about controlling conditions. Issues pertinent to making decisions regarding assessment strategies are reviewed.

The Richards Family

Mrs. Amelia Richards and her son Larry, age 14, were referred for assistance by a school social worker. A precipitous drop in Larry's grades (from a B to a C-minus average) and increases in days absent from school (from an average of one day every other month to 5 days per month) were the reasons for the referral.

The school social worker had spoken to Mrs. Richards on two occasions. The mother said that she was aware of Larry's school problems. Moreover, she said that she had difficulty with her son at home, but felt unable to control him. In the opinion of the school social worker, Larry was at risk of dropping out of school or being expelled.

Mr. Krasky, the agency social worker, met with Mrs. Richards and Larry twice following the referral. (Mrs. Richards had been divorced from her husband for 9 years; she had no knowledge of his whereabouts.)

The mother said that she thought that Larry was headed for trouble, and that she was not able to control him. "Everything had been fine until about a year ago when Larry fell in with a bad crowd," she said. Since then, in addition to his difficulties at school, Larry was staying away from home quite a lot.

Mr. Krasky asked for examples of Larry's behavior that led his mother to say that he was out of her control. She answered in a general manner, substituting terms like "unmanageable" and "undisciplined" for out of control. Changing his line of questioning, the worker asked Mrs. Richards what her son would be doing about his household responsibilities, curfew, school, and his relationship to his friends if he was behaving in an acceptable manner. Mrs. Richards said that Larry would tell her who his friends were, where he was going and how he spent his time, that he would be doing well in school, and that he would "mind" her—for example, that he would come home when she told him to. The mother conceded that she did not know that Larry and his friends were getting into trouble. Rather, she assumed this to be true since her son was secretive about his friends and what they did with their time.

In concluding the interview, the worker asked whether Mrs. Richards thought that some of Larry's behavior—his reluctance to tell her about all of his activities, and his wish to extend curfew beyond the time limits that she set, for example—was normal for a boy of his age who was trying to assert his independence. Mrs. Richards's response was to repeat that she thought that Larry was headed for trouble, to which she added that things had been different when she was growing up.

During the second meeting, Mr. Krasky spoke with Mrs. Richards and Larry separately. The mother contributed little in the way of additional information. Larry, while not denying the situation at school, said that he could make up his grades whenever he felt like it. He did not agree with his mother's suggestion that he was away from home too much. "She thinks that I'm still a baby," he said.

Larry would not discuss his friends or how they spent their time together. He told Mr. Krasky that all that his mother wants is for him to do "what she says, when she says it, and how she says it, period." "If your mother treated you as you think you should be treated, what would be happening?" Mr. Krasky asked. Larry's answer was that his mother would listen to his side of the story and stop nagging him so much.

Speaking to both mother and son, the worker asked whether Larry had considered that he might not graduate or that he might be expelled if his grades continued to fall and absences continued. "They just say that to scare you," Larry said.

Changing the topic of conversation, the worker asked a series of questions about specific areas of family life. He learned that Larry did his household chores, for which he received an allowance of $5 per week. His mother added, however, that he did them only with prodding and not always in a manner she considered thorough. Mother and son spent little time together, save for mealtimes several evenings each week. They did go to monthly family gatherings.

When asked what, if anything, Larry or Mrs. Richards would like to see changed in their lives, the mother said that she would like her son to be a "good boy," as he used to be, and to listen to her and do well in school. Larry said that he liked things the way they were.

Mr. Krasky was frank in stating that he agreed with the school social worker that Larry was at risk of expulsion or of dropping out of school if his current behavior continued. He added that it was possible that the family would be reported to protective services because of Larry's truancy. The possible consequences of such a report, including the chance of juvenile court involvement, were described.

Mr. Krasky concluded the second interview by saying that he would like to see if they could work together toward a satisfactory resolution of Larry's school problem and to see if they could negotiate for some of the freedom the young man seemed to want, in a manner acceptable to Mrs. Richards. Mrs. Richards readily agreed; Larry, reluctantly so.

From these meetings, the worker learned the following:

1. Mrs. Richards was aware of Larry's school problems. Further, she saw her son's behavior at home as problematic and out of her control. Larry, while not denying the situation at school, did not see it as a problem. He did not agree with his mother's view that his behavior at home was troublesome. Instead, he viewed the problem as his mother's nagging.
2. The difficulties identified had begun approximately one year ago and were said to have escalated during the year. No precipitating events were identified. The family had never received any social services.
3. The fact that Larry did his chores, shared some meals with his mother each week, went to family gatherings, and had done well in school in previous years were seen as assets.

Mr. Krasky hypothesized that:

1. Mrs. Richards's expectations of Larry were not realistic for a young man of his age. This was suggested by her statements that her son should mind her at home and by her reference to the way things were when she was growing up. Larry's statement that he was treated like a baby, that his mother wanted total compliance with

her demands, and that she would not listen to him reinforced this hypothesis.

2. Mother and son were forcing each other into a rigid position. Mrs. Richards's demands grew in relation to Larry's unwillingness to rectify his school problems and his refusal to share information about his friends. Larry, for his part, grew more stubborn as his mother's demands increased.

3. Some of the time that Larry spent away from home might be explained as avoidance of what was to him an aversive home environment. His unwillingness to talk about his friends and how they spent their time might be an effort to assert his independence.

4. It was reasonable to assume that the problem would, at best, remain as it was; at worst, it would grow until Larry either dropped out of school or was expelled. And the possibility that Larry might get into trouble with his friends had to be recognized as a legitimate concern.

The hypothesis that would guide the selection of assessment strategies was that the interaction between mother and son had become aversive for reasons noted above. The aversive nature of their interactions was forcing mother and son into rigid and uncompromising positions that exacerbated existing problems. The assessment strategies selected are discussed further on. First, some general issues regarding assessment, highlighted by this case, are reviewed.

Issues in Assessment

The foregoing hypothesis does not explain why Larry's grades were falling nor does it explain his truancy. While speculating that his wish to assert his independence was causal to his behavior, it is reasonable to suggest that information regarding the young man's larger social environment would be relevant for assessment. Answers to questions such as, How does Larry spend his time when truant from school? Who are his friends and in what ways are they maintaining the behaviors causing difficulties at school and at home? could provide relevant information for problem solving. But obtaining accurate information on these issues would require Larry's cooperation, which at this time was minimal. Although it is possible that intervening at the level of the nuclear family would resolve the problems of the Richards family, it was also possible that positive outcomes would not occur, or would be minimal. The worker must be mindful of these limitations and be prepared to develop a strategy for gathering additional assessment information if problem resolution does not occur when problem-solving strategies are implemented based on the information that is available.

Several principles regarding assessment can be culled from this statement. First, all initial decisions as to what will be studied during assessment must be viewed as tentative. Whether the conditions selected for study are the most salient ones will not be known until an effort is made to modify them during intervention and the effects, in terms of problem reduction, are evaluated. Thus, assessment must be viewed as a continuing process. Initial hypotheses about controlling conditions may be incorrect, causing a worker to formulate new hypotheses and search for new information; or hypotheses may be only partially correct. The interaction between Larry and Mrs. Richards may indeed contribute to family difficulties. However, satisfactory resolution of problems may require knowledge of the young man's larger social environment and intervention at that level.

It should be clear then, that antecedent and maintaining conditions may be found in the client's family environment; in the immediate social environment, which includes significant others in the community and work place with whom the client interacts; or in the larger social environment of institutions and the policies and laws that govern access to institutional resources. Thus, the difficulties in the Richards's family could be the result of mother-son interaction (the family environment), and/or Larry's interactions with his peer group (the immediate social environment), and/or interactions between Larry and school personnel (the larger social environment).

The likelihood of identifying the conditions that give rise to and maintain problem behaviors can increase if workers have access to information within and across environments. This is so because the worker will have a broader base from which to seek information and isolate relevant factors.

But a thorough assessment of each of the environments in which a client moves is a difficult task. Workers cannot follow clients around and observe them in every situation. Enlarging the scope of assessment requires greater reliance on client self-reporting and on enlisting the aid of significant others to gather assessment information.

Here, a note of caution is in order. It is not reasonable to seek information about client interactions in a variety of settings unless one has reason to think that the most salient variables lie in the settings to be explored. Gathering information descriptive of client behavior in a variety of settings could produce a voluminous amount of data whose analysis can prove extremely difficult. Before undertaking the tasks involved one should have good reason to think that the information gained is essential to case planning and problem solving. Second, respect for client privacy demands that one limit data-gathering activities to issues that workers can justify by formulating hypotheses to show why the information sought is deemed relevant. Finally, the limits of a worker's ability to effect environmental change must be recognized. It is one thing to show that certain resources are needed to assist clients or that restrictive eligibility standards preclude clients receiving needed services; it is another thing to create new programs or remove restrictive eligibility requirements. Such actions usually require extensive advocacy, the effects of which may not be realizable in time to benefit any one client. And, extensive efforts to change the larger social environment can work against clients if workers spend a disproportionate amount of their time on such activities, thereby not attending to more immediate and more readily solvable problems.

Addressing the issue of systems theories, Carel Germain notes that they "Provide rich insights into what is going on in the . . . client's life space but [are] not yet able to describe what to do about it. . . . Two practice questions that we cannot answer are where, how, and when to intervene in a complex field of systems and what planned and unplanned consequences our interventions are likely to produce" [5:6].

Assessment Strategy

Mr. Krasky wanted information about Mrs. Richards's expectations of Larry and Larry's thoughts about his responsibilities to his mother.* Also, he wanted to learn how mother and son communicated their thoughts and feelings to each other. Whether they were able to have a productive discussion in which each listened to what the other had to say, and whether mother and son had the skills and the willingness to negotiate differences of opinion, were areas of concern.

Mr. Krasky chose to approach assessment of the first issue in three ways. First, he asked mother and son to identify three topics for conversation. Each of the topics selected was to represent an area the discussion of which created friction for mother and son—for example, time that Larry spent away from home or Larry's response to his household responsibilities.

On three separate occasions, the clients were asked to discuss the chosen topics, which were to be taped. To initiate conversation, Mr. Krasky asked Mrs. Richards and Larry to imagine that Larry was going out for the evening. He asked his clients how they would generally approach a discussion of this subject—for example, would Larry say "I'm going out tonight," or would Mrs. Richards, seeing Larry with his coat on, say "Where are you going?" Beginning with the opening comment, the clients were asked to discuss the issue in as customary a manner as possible.

---

*For reasons noted above, the worker determined that efforts to acquire information about Larry's friends and his truancy would not be fruitful at this time. Mr. Krasky asked Larry if he would agree to attend school for 10 days straight, during the assessment period. (Larry said that he would think about it. In fact, he missed only 1 day out of 10). It was Mr. Krasky's intention to have some "casual" conversations with Larry about schooling. He hoped to get some general information about what Larry liked and disliked about school and what career aspirations, if any, he had. The worker hoped to establish a working relationship with the young man that would permit him to address the school issue more directly.

It was the worker's intention to analyze the content of the tape recording, using a predetermined set of categories that would provide information in two areas. The first focused on the *content* of the communication, the second on the *method of delivering* information [10:33–42].

Issues of content direct attention to the wording of a message—for example, expectations stated in a negative or disapproving manner, such as "You never listen to anything that I say." The content of a message may be appropriate but its delivery negative. For instance, Mrs. Richards might say, "I'd like you to come home by 11 P.M.," but deliver the message in a sarcastic manner, implying that Larry couldn't care less about what she wanted.

It was assumed that these conversations would provide information about Mrs. Richards's expectations and Larry's responses, as well as about how mother and son communicated their thoughts and feelings.

The second approach to gathering assessment data required that Mrs. Richards and Larry report their thoughts and feelings in writing immediately following the simulations. Specifically, Mr. Krasky asked them to respond to a checklist containing a series of items with which they could strongly agree, agree, disagree, or strongly disagree. The statements, "This conversation was typical of the way we discuss this subject," "I communicated my thoughts (and feelings) clearly," "My mother (son) understood what I said," "I understood what my son (mother) said," "My mother (son) has no interest in how I feel about this matter," illustrate checklist items.

Finally, using a partially structured interview format, Mr. Krasky spoke with Mrs. Richards and Larry separately to elicit further information on the subjects of concern and to clarify ambiguities from the taped conversations. Examples of structured questions posed to Larry are, "Do you think that you have a responsibility to tell your mother where you are going at night and what you will be doing? If so, how much information do you think it fair to share? If not, why not?" He asked Mrs. Richards whether she thought that young men of Larry's age should participate in making decisions, for example, relative to the time that he came home at night and what was her frame of reference for whatever expectations she held.

Each source of assessment data complements the other while simultaneously offering unique information. Taken together, the information gathered should contribute to selection of problem-solving strategies.

For example, the information from the simulations should provide initial support for, or negation of, the worker's main hypotheses about the relationship between Mrs. Richards's expectations and Larry's behavior. The self-reports following the simulations would indicate whether, in the opinion of both clients, the taped dialogue accurately reflected the manner in which they discussed issues. The structured interviews would permit the worker to expand the data base from the tapes and self-reports, since they provided a way in which the worker could gain clarifying information on vague issues and follow through on selected topics by asking specific questions.

Now, assume that the content of the tapes supports the initial hypotheses and that the client's self-reports indicate that the discussions are accurate representations of how they talk about relevant issues. Analysis of the tapes might indicate differences in either the content or the method of delivering information. The focus of intervention would depend upon which category was of concern: "When dealing with problems of content . . . the focus of intervention may be to establish client acquisition of a positive verbal repertoire, to increase the frequency of existing positive statements and decrease the frequency of disapproving statements, or to arrange the conditions for demonstration of already existing skills" [11:98]. If the problem lies in the method of delivery, intervention would focus on helping the clients to modify their "tone of voice, or the nonverbal cues that accompany the message" [11].

The Innes Family

The Innes family was reported to protective services by a physician at County Hospital. Michael Innes, age 15, had been picked up by the police, who found the boy wandering downtown at 5 A.M. He had a black eye and was limping. During an examination at the hospital emergency room, bruises and lacerations were observed on Michael's upper right arm and shoulder.

The young man would not explain how he had been injured. Michael's father, James Innes, who had been called to come to the hospital, said that he did not know how his son had been hurt. The examining physician said that the boy's injuries had been inflicted, not caused by accidental means such as a fall. But it was not clear who had inflicted the injuries.

Michael was released from the hospital and accompanied home by Janice Cook, a protective service worker. James Innes, his wife Norma, and their 8-year-old daughter, Linda, were at home when Ms. Cook and Michael arrived.

Ms. Cook explained her role as a protective service worker in relation to the state law requiring investigations when injuries such as those sustained by Michael were reported. She described the services offered by the agency and indicated her intention to try to help the family resolve this matter.

Regarding the family's current situation, the worker learned that Mr. Innes had been laid off from his job at a local factory 2 months before the investigation. Mrs. Innes did domestic work to supplement the income from her husband's unemployment insurance. The father had not been successful in finding new work. He spent his days doing repairs on the family home and, as he put it, "just hanging around."

Inquiries into the cause of Michael's injury had been made at the hospital. As noted, explanations were not forthcoming. In the worker's judgment, resuming this line of questioning was not likely to be productive. Although the medical report stated that Michael's injuries could not have been sustained accidentally, given the boy's age, they could have been caused in a fight with other teen-agers. Ms. Cook assumed, because of Michael's silence on the subject of how his injuries occurred and what she described as the father's discomfort during the interview, that the injuries were the result of a fight between father and son. Proving this, however, would be very difficult.

She therefore decided to approach the investigation by asking questions about the circumstances surrounding the injury rather than by asking directly how the injuries were sustained. Specifically, she asked family members to describe how they had spent the day up to the time Michael was picked up by the police. The following summarizes what was learned.

Mrs. Innes had gone to work around 8 A.M. following an argument with her husband over the subject of money and of Mrs. Innes's working. Both subjects were the cause of frequent arguments. The father did not hesitate to say that he disliked the fact that his wife had to work because he could not find a job. But he acknowledged that the money she earned was necessary to sustain the family. His job skills were limited to the factory work he had been doing. The likelihood of being rehired in the foreseeable future was slim, since layoffs were continuing at the factory. And he had not been successful in finding other work, even of an unskilled nature.

Linda had been kept home from school on the day in question because she was running a low-grade fever. She had been "cranky" all day, wanting someone to play with her. Mr. Innes said that he had been annoyed at having to attend to Linda's needs while simultaneously trying to repair the roof of their home. He had awaited his son's return from school with the expectation that the young man would stay with his sister while he went into town to buy materials needed to complete the repair work. Michael had not come home when expected; rather, he had been over 2 hours late. This, according to his father, was typical of the way in which Michael dealt with his responsibilities. (Michael, in a subsequent conversation, said that he came home from school on time except for days when he had basketball practice.) By the time Michael returned, Mr. Innes said that he was "really put out" because it was too late to go to the store. If Linda was sick the next day, he knew that he would have to stay at home again, deferring completion of repairs until Michael came home from school. When asked to describe what had occurred when the young man returned on the day being discussed, the father conceded having yelled at his son. There was no mention of any physical fight.

Talking to both parents, Ms. Cook asked them to describe their general approach to disciplining their children. Mr. Innes quickly responded by saying that they did not hit their kids and had not done so since they were very little.

During a staff meeting that followed the first home visit, Ms. Cook set forth the following hypotheses regarding Michael's injuries. She suspected that Mr. Innes's general frustration at being out of work, his concern over money problems, and his disapproval of his wife's working were worsened by the fight he and his wife had had the morning of the day Michael was injured. Linda's illness and Michael's tardiness in returning from school, coupled with his annoyance at not being able to finish roof repairs, were such that he and Michael got into a physical fight.

Everyone at the staff meeting agreed that the chances of the family acknowledging this was slim since, in response to questions focusing directly on the causes of the young man's injuries, the family seemed to draw together protectively. The possibility that Michael could have been hurt in a fight with other youngsters, although a less plausible hypothesis, was recognized as a possibility.

The likelihood of Michael being at risk of further injury did not seem great for several reasons. First, Ms. Cook surmised that the fact that the case had come to the attention of protective services would act as a deterrent for the father. There were no previous reports and the family's description of events suggested that the father's response to Michael might best be viewed as situational, with a low probability of recurrence. If Michael did sustain further injuries, they would come to the attention of school authorities who were aware of what had happened. Further injuries, or absences from school, would be reported to protective services. Moreover, Michael was due back at the hospital in 10 days for an examination, adding a further check on his physical condition. Finally, the young man was old enough to act on his own behalf should this be necessary.

Rather than trying to sustain an allegation of physical abuse, which would be difficult, if not impossible, absent a confession, the worker decided to offer assistance to the family with a focus on helping the father to manage his feelings of frustration and helping Michael to behave in a responsible manner about his household responsibilities.

Assessment Strategy

If Ms. Cook was to help Mr. Innes learn to manage his feelings of frustration, she had to learn more about his "moods." Specifically, she wanted to learn how often, on a day-to-day basis, his mood was good or bad, and what conditions were most likely to produce positive or negative feelings. Since this issue involved private thoughts and feelings, Mr. Innes would have to be a main source of assessment information.

The father was asked to record his moods on the form shown in figure 2.13. As the instructions state, Mr. Innes was asked to describe his moods by

Figure 2.13   **FORM FOR RECORDING MOODS AND RELATED ACTIVITIES**

	Date	Time of Day	Mood	Activities Including People Present & Thoughts
Example	12/4	9 A.M.	−	1. Fight with wife regarding money
				2. Worry about not finding work
	12/4	11 A.M.	+	1. Spoke to Joe about not finding work. We're all in the same boat.

INSTRUCTIONS   As often as possible during the day and evening, indicate whether your mood is good or bad by placing a (+) in the column under mood for good feelings or thoughts or a (−) for bad feelings or thoughts. Whenever you record your mood, please write down the date; time of day; what you were doing; who was present, if anyone; and what you were thinking.

placing a plus sign in the column headed "Mood" to indicate good feelings, and a minus sign to show negative feelings. Each time he recorded a mood he was asked to note the date and time of day as well as the activity in which he was engaged at the time. The examples provided on the form were given by the client in response to questions from Ms. Cook, when she asked for illustrations of the conditions that affected Mr. Innes's feelings.

Since both parents said that they frequently argued over money matters and Mrs. Innes's work, and since an argument had taken place on the day that Michael was hurt, Mrs. Innes was asked to report disputes between her husband and herself on the form shown in figure 2.14. Following an argument, Mrs. Innes agreed to place a check in the column headed "Argu-

Figure 2.14   **FORM FOR RECORDING ARGUMENTS AND RELATED ISSUES**

	Date	Time of Day	Argument	Issue
Example	12/6	8:30 A.M.	√	1. John said he's sick and tired of staying home all day
				2. Wants me to quit work

INSTRUCTIONS   Any time that you have an argument with your husband, indicate this by placing a check in the column headed "Argument." Indicate the date and time of day and the issue over which there was a quarrel.

ment," and to record the date and time of day as well as the issue that they had quarreled about. The information recorded by Mrs. Innes would be compared to that recorded by her husband. (The parents were asked not to discuss their records.) If Mr. Innes's moods fluctuated in relation to disputes with' his wife, this should show up in his records. Also, comparing the information recorded by both parents would reveal whether they perceived the cause of arguments similarly.

The final area in which the family was asked to record information concerned Michael's return from school each day and his chore-completion behavior. Separate versions of figure 2.15 were developed, one for Michael and one for Mr. Innes.* Each weekday a check was to be placed on the form if Michael came home directly after school. If not, he was to leave this blank, but to explain his tardiness in the "Comments" section of the form. In addition, whether Michael did his chores, whether in the opinion of father and son they were done satisfactorily, and whether there was any discussion about chore completion was to be recorded.

This information should help to clarify whether Mr. Innes's perception that Michael typically avoided his responsibilities, or whether Michael's view that he was responsible, was correct.

We will return to both of these cases in the next chapter, where case planning is discussed.

CRITERIA FOR DECIDING WHETHER TO OPEN A CASE FOR VOLUNTARY SERVICES

In discussing protective services we saw that the existence of credible evidence of maltreatment is a necessary condition for opening a case. The authority to open a case, regardless of parental wishes, is found in each state's child abuse statutes.

The decision whether to provide services that are requested voluntarily hinges on different factors. Some of these, such as eligibility criteria and the availability of the service requested, were discussed in chapter one in the section on voluntary services. Here, we will look at the relationship between agency policy and this decision.

Ideally, families should have access to whatever services are provided through a community's voluntary child welfare programs. The conditions necessary for realizing this ideal—a sufficient number of staff members to handle the volume of requests and the availability of any service in a quantity sufficient to meet consumer demand—are rarely present.

---

*The recording form for Mr. Innes was identical to the one shown here, with two minor exceptions. First, Michael's name was substituted for "you" in the instructions. Second, Mr. Innes was not asked to explain his son's tardiness in coming home.

Figure 2.15 **FORM TO RECORD RETURNING FROM SCHOOL AND CHORE COMPLETION**

	M	T	W	TH	FR	SAT	SUN
CAME HOME RIGHT AFTER SCHOOL							
DID CHORES							
WITH DISCUSSION							
WITHOUT DISCUSSION							
SATISFACTORY							
IF NOT, WHY NOT							
COMMENTS							

INSTRUCTIONS Each weekday, place a check in the column showing the day of the week to indicate whether you came home right after school. If you did not come directly home, explain why in the "Comments" section. (For example: "Went to baseball practice, "Went to the library to study.") For each day, check whether you completed chores with or without discussion. (For example: "My father had to remind me to go to the grocery store.") Place a Yes or No in the column "Satisfactory" to show whether you think that you did chores correctly. If not, indicate what you should have done differently.

There are costs to families if needed services are denied. But there are also costs when agencies try to accommodate more families than their resources allow. One can question, for example, whether clients benefit when the activity level of a worker's caseload is so high as to preclude undertaking the tasks necessary to provide services. And efforts to serve all families when resources are limited can result in not being able to serve families in greatest need. Therefore, criteria for establishing priorities in service requests to ensure that families with the greatest need are not denied assistance are necessary.

Guidelines that provide workers direction for deciding whether to open a case, with the authority to grant or deny services, must be articulated in agency policy. If an agency defines its service mandate broadly—for example, if policy states that voluntary services are available to any family in the community upon request—problems may occur if resources, including child welfare staff, are limited. A service mandate of such scope also fails to recognize that public child welfare agencies are only one of a community's resources for assisting families.* The importance of spelling out the different responsibilities of all community agencies may be overlooked.

Illinois child welfare policy illustrates the kind of guidelines necessary for deciding whether cases are appropriate for voluntary services. Voluntary services are mandated for children who fall into any one of four categories, and guidelines are spelled out for deciding whether to open cases that do not fall into one of the mandated categories.

The categories of children who must be served are as follows:

1. Children under the age of 13 who have been adjudicated delinquent, and their families.
2. Children for whom the department has already had legal responsibility who were subsequently adjudicated delinquent.
3. Minors in need of supervision and their families. Continued service for this population is required even if the child is over 13.
4. Children who violate a court order, and their families.

Criteria for providing services to dependent children and their families who do not fall into one of the foregoing categories require clear evidence that:

1. *Parenting behavior* falls below *minimum standards* such that a *child is likely to be harmed*;

                                    -or-

    a. The conditions of the child's home are such as to suggest that a child is in danger;

                                    -or-

2. The family needs child welfare services to keep the family together or to help them through a crisis that threatens family stability;

                                    -and-

3. It is probable that the provision of the department's services will alleviate the conditions or change the parental conduct that has led to harm or that threatens harm [7].

The first two criteria for serving cases that do not fall into mandated categories closely approximate those required for the provision of protective

---

*There may be communities where the child welfare agency is, in fact, the only resource for helping families. Although refusing assistance when there are no alternative agencies is difficult, one must bear in mind the hypothetical costs of trying to serve all families.

services. But the requirement differs significantly. Workers need not infer an intention to harm a child. The need to allege parental misconduct is thereby eliminated.

The application of these guidelines can be illustrated with reference to the family whose problems are listed on the profile on page 22. The appropriateness of this case for voluntary services can be seen in that the youngster who is diabetic is at risk because she administers her insulin irregularly. The mother, because she is blind, is not able to monitor her daughter's behavior sufficiently to ensure that she takes her medication as she should. The worker's task is to develop a system that increases the probabilities that the youngster will take her insulin in a way that takes into account the mother's limitations.

There are situations in which children may be at risk because parents who are mildly retarded cannot provide a sufficient level of care, in which the limitations, again, are not due to parental fault. Here, workers in voluntary programs may link parents with resources that can make up for deficits in parenting skills while allowing children to remain in their own homes.

Likewise, children may be at risk if the condition of their home is substandard. If parents cannot afford to make needed repairs, an imputation of neglect would be incorrect. But assistance is necessary.

The second criterion is broad, given the difficulty of predicting whether family stability is threatened. Here, workers must apply judgment to the information that is gathered during assessment to formulate a hypothesis regarding the stability of family life. To illustrate this point, assume that assessment data show that the parents spend the majority of their time together quarreling. They have tried, without success, to resolve their problems without seeking professional help, which they are now asking for as a last resort. While not specifically mentioning divorce or separation, both parents express a weariness with their situation and pessimism regarding the future. Whether they will stay together or separate is speculative. It is reasonable, however, in light of the available data, to suggest that the stability of family life is threatened, and to offer services to increase the frequency of positive exchanges between adults, thereby reducing the frequency of family disputes.

The final criterion is noteworthy in that it forces the worker to consider whether there are services that can be offered that directly address the family's problems. In part, the inclusion of this criterion is an effort to reduce the chances that cases will be opened but not served, or underserved. Either possibility exists when, as previously mentioned, caseload size increases to a point at which the amount of activity required to provide services exceeds the time available to the worker, when services needed to assist a family are not available.

The issue of whether services are likely to benefit the family is an important one. There is evidence to suggest that a tendency exists to refer clients for services—counseling, for instance—without a clear comprehension of expected benefits [2:14]. To satisfy this criterion, workers must specify the likely outcomes of client involvement in service programs when they formulate case plans. Specifying outcomes—stating, for example, that "the clients will increase the frequency with which they engage in positive interaction"—directs attention to the question "What is the likelihood that the program selected can achieve this outcome?" Specifying outcomes in observable and measurable terms creates a framework for accountability that increases the chances that services will be selected with caution. When outcomes are stated in vague terms, e.g., "the clients will learn to respond to each other's need for affection," there is no guidance for choosing programs with a high probability of success since criteria for evaluating success are not given.

FOR DISCUSSION

1.   An anonymous reporter telephoned protective services stating that "something was wrong" in the Carmichael home. "Strangers trooped in and out at all hours." The reporter said that she had not seen the children, Bryan, age 5, and Leslie, age 6, for several days.

When the investigative worker arrived at the home he was at first denied entry. Speaking to Mrs. Carmichael through a closed door, the worker explained why he was there and said that he would have to request police assistance to see the children if Mrs. Carmichael would not cooperate. He was subsequently allowed entry to the home.

In his report, the worker noted that he could not complete an interview with the mother, who "dozed off" several times during the meeting. Mrs. Carmichael did not answer the questions the worker posed regarding how the children were being supervised and whether there were relatives or neighbors whom he might ask to come to the home to provide supervision. The worker said that he could arrange for someone to come to the home to help Mrs. Carmichael and he suggested that she see a doctor. Mrs. Carmichael's response was that she wished everyone would "mind their own business."

TASKS

A.   Determine whether the worker should have taken protective custody, sent a caretaker into the home, or left the situation as he found it.

B. Provide a rationale for your decision.

2. In June of 1981, the grandmother of Kathy and Karen Hamilton, ages 8 and 9, reported that they were being left alone during the day while their mother was at work. She was particularly concerned because the children were unsupervised at least 8 hours a day when school was out of session. The grandparent was not able to assume any responsibility for the care of the children.

    The worker making the first home visit found the children playing in their yard. There was no adult in the home. The children said that a neighbor, Mrs. Orban, looked in on them periodically, and they could go to her if any problems arose. When interviewed, Mrs. Orban said that their mother did not believe there was any need for a full-time babysitter and asked her neighbor to check on the children once every 2 hours or so. The children had access to the indoors and to food in the home.

    ### TASKS

    A. Determine whether the worker should have taken protective custody, sent a caretaker into the home, or left the situation as he found it.
    B. Provide a rationale for your decision.
    C. What would you suggest the worker do next?

3. The principal of Madison Elementary School reported a case of suspected physical abuse. She had observed a bruise and cut over the right eye of Sally Wade, age 7. Sally had told two of her teachers that her father had hit her while he was arguing with her mother.

    There were no previous reports on this family. During the home visit, Mr. and Mrs. Wade said that Sally's injury was the result of getting hit by her 9-year-old brother while the children were "scuffling." The parents expressed dismay when told of the report that Sally had made to her teachers.

    The injury did not appear serious to the worker. The parents' story seemed plausible. Sally refused to talk to the worker and her brother was not at home.

    The investigation continued with a visit to the grandmother, who lived nearby and spent much time with the family. She reported that she had never seen Mr. or Mrs. Wade hit their children, had never observed "suspicious" injuries, and the children had never told her that they had been hit or beaten by either parent.

Sally's brother, Jimmy, was seen in school by the worker the next day. He corroborated his parents' story, as did Sally, who was also seen at this time. When asked why she had told her teachers that her father had hit her, Sally said that she had "made up" the story.

TASKS

A. State what the worker should do next.
B. Decide whether there is credible evidence of physical abuse.
C. Explain the rationale for your decision.

DECISIONS AND RATIONALE

1. The children were taken into protective custody. Mrs. Carmichael did not seem able to supervise them nor could she suggest who might be called upon to provide help. If the mother had agreed to the worker's offer to arrange for medical assistance for her and accepted his offer of providing help in the home, he would have arranged for an emergency caretaker. Absent the mother's consent, he deemed the latter course of action inadvisable.

2. The children were not in immediate danger. There was no reason to take protective custody or to send a caretaker into the home. The children had instructions they could follow in case of an emergency, access to the house, and food. The neighbor checked on them throughout the day, as pre-arranged with their mother, thus providing minimal supervision. Certain next steps are necessary, however. Leave a note for the parent describing why you were there and a number for the parent to call as soon as she returns home. Instruct the children to call you if their parent does not come home. Indicate on the note your intention to contact the mother to arrange for a follow-up visit to discuss the report and ongoing arrangements for the children's supervision.

3. A medical examination is necessary to determine the seriousness of the injuries. It is not reasonable, however, to expect that a physician's report will indicate whether the father or the brother was the perpetrator.

The results of the medical examination should be shared with the family and the conflict between their report of how the injury was sustained and the report that Sally made at school should be discussed further. Unless the family changes their story, it is not likely that the question "Who caused the injury?" will be satisfactorily answered.

If the family sticks to its story, especially if Sally maintains that she made up the story told to her teachers, the weight of the evidence would not be likely to support an allegation of abuse.

Services could be offered if there are problems with which the family would like assistance. Given the above, it is not likely that the case would be opened on an involuntary basis.

FOR DISCUSSION

TASK ONE

Develop two problem profiles; one for the Richards family (see page 79) and one for the Innes family (see page 86). Check the accuracy of the profiles that you have developed against the examples that appear in figures 2.16 and 2.17.

TASK TWO

Select a case of your own (or one of your workers') that has recently been opened for services. Using this case, complete tasks three through six, below.

TASK THREE

Develop a problem profile.
Order the priorities of the problems and provide a rationale for the priorities set.
Select one problem for assessment.

TASK FOUR

Design a strategy for assessment.
Present a rationale for the procedures chosen.
Design one form for client self-monitoring.

Figure 2.16 PROBLEM PROFILE—RICHARDS FAMILY

Problem No.	Label	Who Labels	Who Has the Problem	Date	Examples	Situation	Assets
1.	Low grades	School Social Worker	Larry		Dropped from B to C average	At school, for the last year	Larry has done well in school in prior years
2.	Truancy	School Social Worker	Larry		Unexcused absences 5 out of 25 days per month	At school, for the last year	Larry attended school regularly prior to this time
3.	Larry out of control —unmanageable	Mrs. Richards (mother)	Mother & Larry		1. Larry stays away from home too much	At home, for the last year	Larry does household chores for his allowance
					2. Larry doesn't mind her—doesn't come home when he's supposed to		Mother & Larry spend some meal times together each week
					3. Larry doesn't tell her where he is going, what he is doing, and who he is spending his time with		Mother & Larry go to monthly family gathering

Problem No.	Label	Who Labels	Who Has the Problem	Date	Examples	Situation	Assets
4.	Larry treated like a baby	Larry	Mother		1. Mother wants Larry to "do what she says, when she says it, & how she says it, period" 2. Mother does not listen to his side of a story 3. Mother nags Larry	At home—primarily in regard to his school problems and spending time with his friends	None identified

TASK FIVE

List the antecedent and maintaining conditions for the problem identified.

TASK SIX

Identify the risk(s) to the child(ren) if the problem is not resolved.

Figure 2.17 **PROBLEM PROFILE—INNES FAMILY**

Problem No.	Allegation	Suspected Antecedents	Who Identified Antecedents	Examples of Antecedents	Problems Identified by Family
1	Physical abuse	1. Father's frustration at being unemployed Concern about money and disapproval of wife working	Protective service worker	1. Mr. & Mrs. I argue about money & Mrs. I working on day that Michael was injured	1. Frequent arguments about money and Mrs. I working
		2. Annoyance with son for coming home late from school	Protective service worker	2. Mr. I was angry with Michael who came home late from school. Verbal fight ensued.	2. Michael is irresponsible

REFERENCES

1. Creative Associates. *Child Protection Services: Inservice Training for Supervisors and Workers.* Developed for the National Center on Child Abuse and Neglect, U.S. Dept. of Health and Human Services. Washington, D.C., n.d. See for a more detailed statement on evidence.
2. Eileen D. Gambrill, and Kermit T. Wiltse. "Foster Care: Plans and Activities." *Public Welfare* 32 (Spring 1974).
3. Eileen D. Gambrill, and Theodore J. Stein. *Supervision in Child Welfare: A Training Manual.* Berkeley, CA: University of California Extension Press, 1978. See for evaluation and assessment strategies.
4. Eileen D. Gambrill. *Behavior Modification: Handbook of Assessment, Intervention, and Evaluation.* San Francisco, CA: Jossey-Bass Publishers, 1977.
5. Carel B. Germain. "Introduction: Ecology and Social Work." In Carel B. Germain, ed., *Social Work Practice: People and Environments—An Ecological Perspective.* New York: Columbia University Press, 1979.
6. Walter W. Hudson. "A Measurement Package for Clinical Workers." Paper presented at the Council on Social Work Education, 23rd Annual Program Meeting, Phoenix, AZ, March 1, 1977.
7. Illinois Register. Illinois Department of Children and Family Services. Text of Proposed Rule. Subchapter A: Service Delivery: Part 304, *Access to and Eligibility for Child Welfare Services.*
8. James V. McConnell. *Understanding Human Behavior.* 2nd edition. New York: Holt, Rinehart and Winston, 1977.
9. Walter Mischel. *Personality and Assessment.* New York: John Wiley & Sons, Inc., 1968.
10. G. R. Patterson; J. B. Reed; R. R. Jones; and R. E. Conger. *A Social Learning Approach to Family Intervention.* Vol. 1. *Families with Aggressive Children.* Eugene, OR: Castalia Publishing Co., 1975.

Behavioral Examples if Different from Antecedents	Who Has the Problem Identified by Family	Date	Situational Context for Problem Identified by Family	Family Assets
See #1—example of antecedents	Mr. & Mrs. Innes		At home	Family seems to be close, protective of each other
1. Michael typically comes home late 2. Does not complete chores	Michael		Home	

11. Theodore J. Stein, and Eileen D. Gambrill. *Decision Making in Foster Care: A Training Manual.* Berkeley, CA: University of California Extension Press, 1976.
12. Theodore J. Stein. *Social Work Practice in Child Welfare.* Englewood Cliffs, NJ: Prentice-Hall, Inc., 1981.

Chapter Three

PHASE III:
SERVICE PLANNING

GOAL

Negotiate a Written Service Agreement with Clients

DECISIONS

Both Services   What Is the Appropriate Case Goal?

What Are Appropriate Case Objectives and Tasks?

What Are Appropriate Problem-Solving Strategies?

THE GOAL OF this phase of intake is to formulate a case plan that identifies the permanency goal for a child and describes how the goal will be realized. Case plans are formulated as written service agreements that provide a framework for service delivery and future decision making. The contents of an agreement give direction to the transactions that must occur between clients and practitioners. The procedures described here apply to both protective and voluntary service programs.

Written case plans are required by federal law and the statutes and policies of most states [9]. They should be formulated within 30 days of the time a case is open to the agency.

This chapter begins with a description of the information contained in written service agreements. An array of services that workers use to assist clients in problem resolution are described and guidelines for selection of service strategies are given. We also address issues such as modifying agreements when case circumstances change and monitoring client compliance with service plans. Examples of written agreements are shown. The case planning process is outlined in figure 3.1.

THE CONTENTS OF WRITTEN SERVICE AGREEMENTS

The names of all persons with responsibility for carrying out the case plan, including the agency affiliation of professionals, are reported. The children whose future is the subject of the plan are named even if they are too young to have responsibilities for carrying out the plan.

The statement, "This plan is entered into between Michael Castle, Protective Service Worker for the Briar County Department of Social Services, and Mr. and Mrs. Clyde Fitch, biological parents of Stephen and Emily Fitch, currently in the custody of the Briar County Department of Social Services," illustrates how the parties to the plan are identified.

Case Goals

Case goals describe the overall purpose in working with a family. Workers consult with clients and supervisors when goals are identified and they refer to agency policy for any directives contained therein.

When plans are first formulated, the goal should reflect the social and legal preference for the right of biological parents to retain *or* regain care, custody, and control of their children. If parents cannot or will not work toward this end, the goal selected should give preference to placement of children in the most legally binding relationship. Case goals, in descending order of preference, are to: (1) maintain children in their own homes; (2) reunite children in foster care with their biological parents; (3) terminate parental rights with subsequent adoption or court appointment of a legal guardian; (4) plan for long-term foster care, with relatives if possible; and (5) plan for independent living for young people age 16 or older for whom placement in a family home is not appropriate.

Figure 3.1 THE CASE PLANNING PROCESS

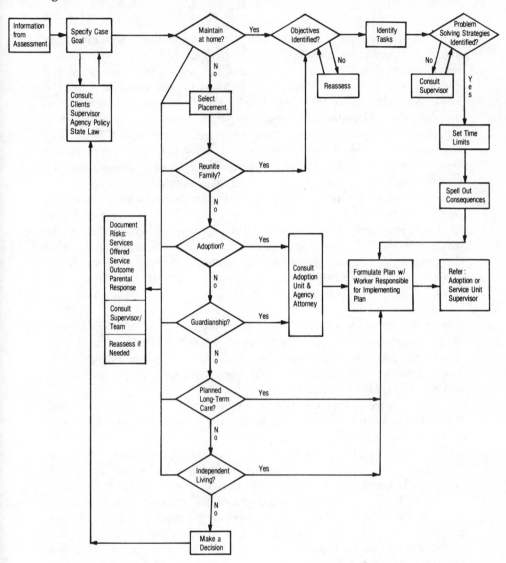

Movement down the hierarchy should be justified with evidence showing why the preferred goal cannot be pursued (see fig. 3.1). For example, justification for placing children in foster care should be supported by evidence showing that children are at risk if left at home, with documentation of services provided to reduce risk (or evidence that parents will not accept services), and the outcome of service provision.*

---

*Such detailed documentation cannot, of course, be gathered when placement occurs under emergency conditions.

Selection of a case goal can be difficult because of the hypothetical risks involved (for example, questions such as whether a child will be safe if left in her own home or if returned home), and has serious implications for the entire family, particularly when the decision is to place children out of the home. An unwillingness to engage in risk taking may cause a worker to avoid decisions. But risk taking is an inevitable part of selecting options, since one cannot predict the long-term consequences of choices made. A worker's willingness to take risks may increase if responsibility for decision making is shared with others. Thus, the importance of joint decision making involving clients, supervisors, and/or team members is highlighted.

Decisions regarding a child's future living arrangements should give preference to the wishes of parents and children: "By putting a client's [preference] in writing and by delineating the responsibility of each party involved in the [agreement] each person is recognized as an integral part of the process of problem resolution . . . signing a [written agreement] can increase a client's commitment to participate in efforts to make change" [7:26].

Workers should know that there is little to be gained from efforts to assess whether parents are motivated to follow through with a plan. Whatever staff members think about whether clients will realize their goals, they should be given the opportunity to do so. Their involvement or lack of involvement in following through with the conditions set forth in the plan will attest to their motivation.

Client choice in goal selection may be constrained. A parent may want her child placed out of the home. Agency policy may preclude this option absent evidence that the child is in danger in her own home and that the danger cannot be reduced with at-home services. Such evidence may not exist. Here, the worker's main task is to explain why the client's wishes cannot be honored and to offer services to reduce or eliminate those family problems that led to the request for placement. One hopes that problem resolution will increase the willingness of family members to remain together.

When parents and children are not sure whether they wish to live together, the case goal may be to reach a decision. Here, a permanency decision is held in abeyance for 60 to 90 days. The rationale for this position is that a decision to have a child removed or a negative stance on family reunification may be influenced by the severity of problems.

For example, there are situations in which a child has been in care for several years and parent-child visits have been few and far between. Visits, when they do occur, may be unpleasant because both the parent and child lack the skills necessary to engage in positive interaction. If worker attention focuses on increasing skills in areas where deficiencies are identified, the family may reach a decision to reunite.

Problem-Solving Objectives

Problem-solving objectives must be established for each of the difficulties that has to be resolved to reach the case goal. Objectives should be reported in observable and measurable terms that describe what the client will be doing differently or what changes are expected in a client's circumstances when problems are resolved. When the goal is to maintain children at home or to reunite those in foster care with their biological families, the process of formulating objectives is informed by assessment data in which the risks that face children are reported. When adoption or guardianship is being pursued, objectives often focus on resolving legal issues—for instance, compiling the documentation needed to pursue termination of parental rights, finding an adoptive home, and assisting the child and caretaker in preparing for their new relationship.

All of the information describing outcomes may be reported in the case objective, or the weight of specificity may be distributed across the objective and tasks. (Tasks are discussed on page 110.) The former is appropriate when outcomes can be achieved through activities occurring at a single point in time—for example, if one is asking a client to sign up for food stamps, to enroll a child in day care, or to take a child for a medical examination. One must test whether the client has the skills and resources necessary to meet the objective—for instance, ensure that the client is able to fill out an application form and has a Medicaid card or the means to pay for a medical exam. If deficits exist, tasks describing how the client is to acquire skills or resources must be spelled out. (See page 110.)

Problem resolution frequently requires a series of actions by worker and client over time. Visiting between parents and their children in foster care and helping clients to acquire new child care skills or to modify expectations of children are issues of this sort. Here, the objective may be phrased in more general terms, such as to increase the frequency of positive interactions between a client and his 8-year-old son. Specific information about frequency and defining positive interaction can be reported in the steps that must be undertaken to realize the objective. Examples of this are offered further on where written service agreements are presented.

The importance of formulating objectives so that outcomes can be observed and measured cannot be overstated. Clients have a right to know what will be different in their lives as a function of involvement with the child welfare agency. Vague objectives undermine this right and increase the chances for misunderstandings between worker and client regarding expected outcomes. The statement, "Mr. and Mrs. Brown will find adequate housing," is an example of a vague objective since "adequate" means different things to different people. A more appropriate objective might be, "Mr. and Mrs. Brown will rent a two-bedroom apartment with the plumbing in working order."

Client involvement in service delivery programs may increase when they know what to expect as a function of their involvement. And clearly formulated goals provide a yardstick against which change can be evaluated. As we shall see later, they facilitate the selection of problem-solving strategies.

To establish problem-solving goals and to select problem-solving strategies, workers must identify the behaviors, thoughts, or feelings that are *incompatible* with those creating difficulties. *Physically incompatible* behaviors are those that cannot be performed at the same time as problem behaviors. If a client is preparing three nutritionally balanced meals each day, arranging for supervision when she is away from the home, or disciplining a child using noncorporal methods of punishment, she cannot simultaneously be neglecting her child's nutrition or supervision, nor will there be a risk of abuse from excessive use of corporal punishment.

Behaviors to reduce or eliminate problems may be *functionally* rather than physically incompatible. If a client does not feel depressed when she spends time with other adults, contact with other adults can be increased to reduce depression.

Physically incompatible behaviors, then, are the opposite of problem behaviors. Their identification follows from information regarding skill and knowledge deficits. Functionally incompatible behaviors are often hinted at, indirectly, by clients. Recall the recording form for Mr. Innes where an example of a positive mood was related to speaking with a friend. If further evidence confirms the relationship between positive feelings and talking with others, the frequency with which the father engages in the latter type of behavior can be increased as a way of decreasing his negative affect.

Difficulties in identifying objectives are often the result of incomplete assessment. If a worker cannot describe changes in observable and measurable terms, he must consider the possibility that he may have to repeat a part or parts of the assessment process. Behavior change that is reported in problem-solving goals may be described in one of six ways:

> (1) the *acquisition* of new skills (learning new job skills or new child care skills); (2) the *increase* in desirable behaviors (in the frequency with which parents and children have positive interactions); (3) the *decrease* of undesirable behaviors (to reduce the frequency of negative statements exchanged by parent and child); (4) the *elimination* of undesirable behavior (drug use); (5) the *maintenance* of desired behavior at a specified rate (continued positive interaction); or, (6) the *variation* of behavior (increasing the variety of ways a person may initiate play activities with a child.) [7:17–18].

The following are examples of clearly stated objectives:

Mr. King will acquire and demonstrate skills at using noncorporal methods of discipline.

Ms. Johnson will have a minimum income needed to sustain her children (approximately $300 per month) either through employment or application for receipt of an AFDC grant within 60 days.

John will be attending the Stay Put Day Care Center between the hours of 9 A.M. and 1 P.M. within 30 days.

Mr. Donaldson will develop a plan of activities for himself and his son 2 weeks before the trial visit scheduled to begin on May 17th.*

Workers should take pains to ensure that the wording of objectives reflects the outcome desired. The statement "Johnny will attend school Monday through Friday, from 9 A.M. to 3 P.M." is not appropriate if the intention is to help Johnny improve his grades. The problem with this objective is that the client can meet the expectation, i.e., he can attend school according to the goal statement, but not attain the principal objective of better grades. Appropriately written, the wording of the objective should describe what the problem situation will look like when the problem is resolved (e.g., Johnny will have attained at least a C average in school). The activities that the worker and teacher assume are necessary to increase the youngster's grades, such as attending certain classes, writing a specified number of pages each day, or reading a specified number of pages each day, are reported as a series of tasks.

Consider a further example. If a client is using drugs but the drug use is not incapacitating, the objective in a case plan should describe the changes necessary to safeguard the child—for example, changes in the parent's methods of child care or supervision. If an objective indicates only that the client will not use drugs, it fails to identify what the client will be doing to protect the child's safety.

A useful way to evaluate whether the objective is worded appropriately is to ask the question, "Would I be willing to dismiss protective services or to return a child from care when the conditions specified are met?" If skill or knowledge deficits were instrumental to an act of maltreatment, the cessation of drug use will not, ipso facto, ensure the child's safety. Thus, the worker must determine what changes are necessary to protect the youngster. Failure to address issues of safety may alter the worker's perception of the risk involved in dismissing protective services or in returning children from care.

Objectives should be written in positive language, describing the behaviors to be increased or acquired rather than those to be decreased or eliminated. It is often easier to decrease undesired behavior by increasing

---

*The skills that Mr. King is to acquire or the activities that Mr. Donaldson is to identify are described in specific terms in the tasks that are written for the objective (see p. 110).

desired behavior. And unless efforts are made to help clients acquire positive skills for coping with their problems, the client is apt to continue to engage in the undesired behavior.

There are situations in which assessment will not be complete within 30 days. One's work schedule may preclude visiting clients as often as necessary, needed assistance with assessment tasks may not be readily available, or a resource person may state that he needs additional time to complete assessment tasks.

Should this occur, the written service agreement can be formulated so that the main objective gives structure to the assessment process.* For example, in a protective service case in which the child is at home, the objective may be to complete assessment tasks within 30 days by worker observation of parent-child interaction during regularly scheduled worker visits; or to complete assessment tasks by having the client meet with Ms. Smith, public health nurse, once a week for 3 weeks. If a child is in care, the objective may establish a schedule for parent-child visits and indicate the worker's intention to observe parent-child interaction during a set number of visits.

When the objective of a service agreement is completion of assessment tasks, the overall time frame should be brief, 30 to 45 days at most. The agreement should include a statement that it will be amended when assessment is completed, the amendment describing the specific changes necessary to realize the long-range case goal. (Amending service agreements is discussed on pages 122 through 123.)

Tasks

For each problem-solving objective the tasks that must be undertaken to reach the objective are described. When collaterals are going to assist clients in problem solving, the child welfare worker's responsibility is to set forth a general framework for client involvement and a method for case coordination. For example, if the objective is to increase a parent's skills at noncorporal methods of punishment, and the strategy to achieve this is for the client to attend parenting classes, tasks would describe: (1) the frequency with which the client is expected to attend classes (every Monday night, beginning April 5th, from the hours of 7 to 9); (2) the duration of classes (for a period of 3 months); (3) a framework for exchange of information between a child welfare worker and the person conducting the parenting classes (Ms. Young, child welfare worker, will telephone Ms. Thomas at the Parent Edu-

---

*Completion of assessment tasks may be the only objective, or it may be one of several. Additional objectives, describing outcomes for problems where assessment is complete, may be included.

cation Center once each week to ascertain client progress in the educational program); (4) the role of the worker as mediator should any difficulties arise in client attendance or participation (Ms. Young agrees to convene meetings, if needed, for the purpose of resolving any difficulties in client attendance and participation in classes); and (5) if the court is involved, a framework for providing information needed for court reporting is established. For example: "Ms. Young is responsible for gathering information necessary for court reporting and for filing a report with the court, including recommendations regarding the future living arrangements of Jeanne Hyde. Ms. Smith of the Hillside Community Mental Health Center agrees to present a written progress report at least 5 days before the court hearing of July 5th."

The exact process to be followed in assisting the client to acquire new skills should be described by the collateral resource. If the child welfare worker assumes responsibility for assisting clients in resolving their problems, the worker describes the procedures to be followed. For instance, the worker may report a method whereby he will model desired behaviors (bathing or feeding an infant), following which the client will be asked to rehearse the behaviors observed. The worker then offers performance feedback to the client, who is given the chance to repeat the behaviors.

Tasks should build upon a client's assets as listed on the problem profile. Problem-solving tasks, in essence, describe a method for bridging the gap between a client's present skills or assets and those she is expected to demonstrate when problem resolution has been attained. For example, if a client is visiting a child in foster care once each month for 1 hour, this schedule of visiting is the client's current asset. If the objective is for a child to spend a 4-day trial visit prior to restoration, the worker must describe a series of steps that increases the frequency and duration of visits from the once-a-month schedule to the 4-day-trial visit.

When tasks are put in writing and linked to time frames for their accomplishment, they can be useful in identifying the point at which a program fails. This is especially important if worker-client contacts are infrequent. Using the previous example, the client who is visiting once a month for 1 hour may increase her visits to once a week for 3 hours and then stop visiting. Information regarding the point at which the client ceased visiting can serve as a cue to the worker whose task it is to identify and remove obstacles to fulfilling the case objective. The client may lack the skills needed to engage her child in positive interaction for more than 3 hours. The worker's task is to increase the client's skill level in order to continue with the visiting program.

Tasks should be accelerated in small increments. Generally, it is preferable to increase visits from 1 to 2 hours per week than from 1 to 4 hours. This is so because large increments may require activities that go beyond a client's skills, increasing the chances of client failure. It is easier to accelerate tasks when a client is doing well than it is to back up and start over if failure has occurred. And small increments may increase the chances that clients will have successful experiences. This can be especially important for clients who have been in the child welfare system for long periods of time and who have a history of failure in achieving their goals.

Finally, tasks with accompanying time frames can be used as a checklist by a client. A visiting schedule or schedule of appointments with a counselor or worker can be taped to a refrigerator or cabinet door and used as a reminder of appointments. Tasks can be checked off as they are completed.

Time Limits

Time limits for attaining goals and objectives of a case plan are reported. Overall time limits are derived from consideration of the length of time needed to resolve whatever problem will take the longest. Thus, if there are four problem-solving objectives and one requires 7 months to realize, the 7-month period of time can be used as the overall time frame for obtaining the long-range case goal.

Consequences

Clients have a right to know the likely outcome of their involvement or noninvolvement in case-planning activities. Consequences will differ on a case-by-case basis. If a child is at home and if the consequence of parental failure to modify behavior is that the child will have to be removed, this should be stated in the plan. Likewise, if parental failure to visit a child in care is that termination of parental rights will be considered, this, too, should be reported. When the court is involved, given that the worker cannot ensure that a member of the bench will accept his recommendations, consequences should be written as "The worker will recommend to the court that Mary Harvey be returned to the home of her biological parents," or "The worker will consult with counsel regarding the possibility of termination of parental rights."

The information described above is formulated into a written service agreement. If agency procedure dictates that different workers formulate and implement the plan, the worker who will bear responsibility for carrying out the agreement should, whenever possible, be involved in the planning process. Once the plan is formulated, the case is transferred to the worker (or supervisor) who will be responsible for implementing the agreement.

The signatures of each person who is a party to the plan are the last items included.

Multiple Uses of Service Agreements

Written service agreements may be used to clarify any arrangement between two or more parties [7:25]. Thus, in addition to reporting long-range case goals, agreements may focus on short-term arrangements (clarifying expectations of parents, children, and workers for a 1-week trial visit); they may be formulated between two clients (describing a method for dividing responsibilities for household chores); or between two workers (for the purpose of coordinating service delivery) [2:151–161]. And written agreements may be used between worker and foster parents, in which long-range goals for a child who will remain in foster care are described.

SELECTING PROBLEM-SOLVING STRATEGIES

The process of establishing objectives requires consideration of how they will be realized. This proceeds on knowledge of resources available and of the different purposes that each resource can fulfill. And in selecting service strategies one must take into account the fact that people learn differently. Thus, an approach that enables one client to resolve her problems may not be of use to another client with similar problems. Three topics are addressed in the following pages. First, a variety of resources and the ways in which they can be used are reviewed. Next, the subject of differential learning strategies is discussed in the context of methods that counselors use to effect change. Criteria for selection of problem-solving strategies are then presented.

In reviewing the following material, there are several points that the reader should bear in mind. There is often more than one way to realize any problem-solving objective. Parents may acquire new child care skills by attending and participating in parent education classes or by working with teaching homemakers, visiting public health nurses, or child welfare staff members. A single service can be used to meet more than one objective. Parenting classes may offer the opportunity to learn new child care skills or methods of family planning, or they may offer training in money management. Finally, many of the services workers use can be employed to prevent placement as well as to facilitate family reunification. Thus, a protective service worker may ask a parent to enroll a child in day care to reduce stress caused by continual child care responsibilities in order to prevent placement. Enrolling a child in day care may be a condition for family reunification when a single parent is employed, or if it is necessary to offer a child educational experiences that the parent is not able to provide.

Parent education is a preventive measure, since children may be at risk of abuse or neglect if their parents lack child care skills or have deficits in knowledge. For example, a parent may not know how to discriminate between physical conditions that can be ministered to at home versus those that require medical attention.

Parent education classes can provide learning experiences in a variety of areas, including basic child care skills and noncorporal methods of discipline. Education to modify a parent's misperceptions of age-appropriate behavior, to increase a parent's knowledge of nutrition and meal planning, of money management, or of family planning may be offered. Parent education may be provided in formal classroom settings or in the client's own home by a visiting public health nurse, teaching homemaker, or child welfare worker.

Respite services provide parents with relief from continual child care responsibilities. The use of respite services may reduce stress on a single parent with sole responsibility for child care, thus decreasing the likelihood of maltreatment. The programs described next may offer respite as a primary or secondary service.

Foster care, in its professional conception, was meant to provide respite for parents during crisis periods or times of stress. While a child was in care, services were to be provided to assist parents in resolving their problems, subsequent to which the child was to be returned to her own home. Unfortunately, foster care has become an end in itself rather than a means to the end of helping families resolve problems and regain custody of their children.

Homemakers offer an array of services. If a parent is physically ill, depressed, or experiencing stress to the extent that she ceases to care for her children, a homemaker may assume full-time or part-time responsibility for household management, thereby reducing the need to place children out of the home.

Homemakers with special training may gather assessment data for workers or assume responsibility for teaching parents household management or child care skills. The unique contribution of a homemaker lies in recognizing that because the person is present in the family home, often for long periods of time, she has the opportunity to observe parents and children and to acquire data descriptive of their interactions that workers may not be able to gather. And the presence of a homemaker over time provides a rare opportunity to observe whether parents have acquired and can maintain child care skills taught in formal parent education classes.

Day care offers "full or part-time care for preschool children outside of their homes on a regular basis during the day while their parents work or are engaged in other activities which separate them from their children" [10:1]. Day care may be custodial or educational in nature, or offer opportunities to enhance child development.

Shelters and crisis nurseries provide respite for parents and a safe haven for children who must be removed from their homes at times of extreme family stress. Protective service workers may use these facilities when children have to be temporarily removed subsequent to an investigation. Child care is generally offered for a brief period of time, often no more than 48 hours, following which the child is either returned to her own home or placed in a foster care facility for a time-limited period.

Crisis counseling provided through "hot-lines" or by counselors who visit clients in their own homes can be a valuable resource for parents experiencing stress. Crisis services are predicated on the assumption that risk can be reduced if parents can discuss their feelings and thoughts with an empathic person at the time of the crisis. Thus, if clients are taught to identify when their feelings reach a point where the likelihood of maltreatment increases and to use crisis services at such times, the risk of abuse or neglect may decrease. The worker's comfort in leaving children in their own homes may increase.

Self-help groups such as SCAN (Suspected Child Abuse and Neglect) and Parents Anonymous have come to play an important role in assisting parents who have abused or neglected their children. Their membership is generally made up of persons whose experiences are similar to those they seek to help. Self-help groups may offer a variety of services. Some operate hot-lines and parent education classes and may provide crisis home visits and organize parents who live close to each other to trade off babysitting to provide respite from full-time child care responsibilities.

Counseling is often used as a referral resource for clients who have abused or neglected their children.* Counselors adhere to different schools of thought** regarding human behavior and how change is best approached. Methods employed may come from social learning theory, ego psychology, systems and ecological theories, and communications theory, to mention a few: "Therapy may be offered on a one-to-one basis or in groups, the unit of attention may be the individual or the family, services may be provided solely in the therapist's office, almost totally in the client's natural environment or in both. Treatment may be long-term or time limited, the counselor a professional or lay person" [8].†

It is beyond the scope of this manual to discuss all of the methods counselors use to effect change. However, all approaches fall into one of four categories [2:136–144]: (1) verbal methods, (2) simulations, (3) direct interventions, and (4) instigations or the use of homework assignments. A review of these methods will facilitate understanding of how practitioners undertake

---

*In general, the terms *counseling* and *therapy* may be viewed as synonymous.

**Some counselors practice from a single theoretical perspective while others are eclectic, employing a range of methods according to what seems appropriate for the problem and the client.

†Professional counselors hold advanced degrees in social work, psychology, or psychiatry, for example. Lay counselors are persons whose experiences are similar to those with whom they work. Former child abusers and former drug addicts, for example, may provide lay counseling. Lay counselors often work with clients in their own homes, offering ongoing, nurturing relationships. They often assist parents with practical matters, such as providing transportation for hospital visits. They may, acting as role models, provide instruction in household management and child care skills.

to modify client behaviors, thoughts, and feelings. As noted above, clients learn in different ways. Differences must be taken into account if problems are to be resolved through the use of counseling techniques. In the following review, some of the assumptions regarding how people learn are highlighted.

Verbal methods are frequently used to effect change with individuals and small groups. A main assumption underlying the use of verbal techniques is that clients possess the skills necessary to employ alternatives described or to translate verbal insights into overt behaviors. Problems may result when verbal methods are used but client skill is not assessed. And there is reason to question whether changes taking place in a counselor's office will generalize to the client's natural environment.

A strength of verbal approaches is that clients can be aided in conceptualizing their difficulties and in identifying alternative ways of approaching problem resolution.

Simulations, where workers replicate real-life situations, may be used in the client's natural environment or in instructional settings. **Direct interventions** in the client's natural environment take advantage of situations as they naturally occur, rather than trying to create them, as with simulations. Both methods rest on the assumption that people learn best through direct observation of behaviors to be acquired, the opportunity to replicate what was observed, and to receive performance feedback.

Using either method, the practitioner assesses the client's skills in the area of concern, then develops a program to build on the client's current skills. For example, a worker may observe a parent interact with her 4-year-old and determine that the client's repertoire of skills for positive interaction is limited. The client may exhaust available alternatives after 30 minutes of play. The worker's task is to identify a range of mutually rewarding activities. Next, playing the role of mother, for example, he demonstrates alternative ways of engaging a child in play activities. Following a period of observation, the client is asked to rehearse what was observed, receives feedback on her performance from the worker, and is given the opportunity to try again.

Client comfort may be greater during simulations than when practice takes place under naturally occurring conditions. The chances that behavior change will generalize, relative to the use of verbal methods, is increased, since practice takes place under conditions that approximate those in the client's own environment. However, behavior displayed during simulations may not be representative of behaviors displayed under normal conditions.

Both simulations and direct interventions, because they afford the client the opportunity to practice new skills, to receive feedback, and to try again, may increase the chances that new skills will be learned. This is in contrast to verbal methods, which rely on a discussion of skills but do not afford an opportunity for practice.

Homework assignments or instigations to undertake certain activities outside the office may be given to clients. A parent and youngster may be given the chance to practice new ways of negotiating problem resolution during a simulation and asked to practice the skills worked on in the office. Practice in the client's own home increases the likelihood that changes will generalize to and be maintained in settings where the use of skills acquired is most pertinent.

A Note on the Selection of Counseling Programs

Child welfare staff members must seek information describing the methods used by counselors to whom they refer clients. Referrals are made too often without a clear comprehension of the techniques counselors use. Client discomfort with counseling methods may cause them to withdraw from programs. This can result in blaming the client, who is seen as lacking motivation for change. In fact, the problem may be due to the worker's failure to attend to the fit between counseling methods used and different learning patterns.

One must not assume that all counselors are able to deal with any problem presented by a client. Practitioners often specialize, having expertise in marital counseling, for instance, but not in drug abuse counseling. Clearly formulated objectives that describe what the client will be doing following completion of a counseling or training program, or that describe changes in a client's circumstances, can be used to open dialogue with counselors as to whether they are able to bring about desired change.

Collateral resources must be willing to work toward the changes established by child welfare staff. Bear in mind that the main purpose in providing child welfare services is to increase a parent's skills or knowledge to a minimum level necessary to stabilize family life. Once accomplished, the child welfare agency may withdraw from the case. The client, if she chooses, can pursue counseling voluntarily, seeking more global change goals that aim to improve the overall quality of life. Counselors involved in child welfare cases must be educated to the limited purpose of child welfare services and they must be willing to work toward the objectives established by workers, clients, and the courts.

Collaterals, then, must be both able and willing to work toward the changes described in case plans. In addition, they must agree to do so within the time limits established and not to subordinate objectives they have agreed to pursue to other agendas; they must also be willing to provide information needed for decision making and court reporting.

GUIDELINES FOR SELECTING SERVICE STRATEGIES

Services are in short supply in most areas of the country. Therefore, workers are often constrained in selecting programs to assist clients in problem solving. One should, however, have a framework for evaluating programs. First, it makes little sense to use a service simply because it exists. Workers should have reason to think that the programs chosen will help to solve client problems.* Second, as should be clear from the preceding review of service strategies, there is more than one way to bring about change. Guidelines for selecting services can facilitate the choice of programs most likely to achieve stated objectives. Finally, a worker's understanding of why some interventions do not have the intended effects can be furthered by applying guidelines presented here. This, in turn, can be used as an aid in selecting alternative ways of bringing about change.

When a full range of services is not available, child welfare staff should record the service of choice as well as the service used, and indicate why the former was deemed appropriate. In so doing, staff members evidence their knowledge of how best to approach problem resolution. Unfortunately, workers often record only the services used. To a person reviewing a case record, this can suggest a lack of knowledge on the worker's part of how best to go about solving problems. For example, we know that children have been placed in foster care when the contents of the case record suggest that they could have been kept at home with the use of day care or homemaker services [3:62–80]. Whether the latter were ever considered, however, is often not known. And information regarding services needed but not available can provide information useful for program-funding decisions.

(1) *The service selected should be effective for reducing or eliminating identified problems.* Workers should be familiar with the methods used by collateral resources and with the clinical and research literature describing the effectiveness of intervention methods and the particular problems for which these methods are reported to be useful.

This is necessary in order to evaluate the likelihood that the intervention method chosen will help to realize objectives. The lack of empirical evidence for service effectiveness does not mean that a service is not useful. It does, however, suggest caution in claims made for effectiveness. And a lack of evidence reinforces the importance of continued monitoring of client progress (see page 128) and a willingness to search for new problem-solving strategies when progress in solving problems is not shown.

(2) *There should be evidence that the service is needed.* Workers bear the responsibility for establishing a connection between the services they rec-

---

*Evidence exists that services are often used without a clear understanding of how the program will aid in problem resolution [1:14].

ommend or require and problems identified during assessment. Failure to show why services are required may constitute unnecessary intrusion into family life. The process of selecting services is facilitated when objectives are written in positive language and outcomes reported in observable and measurable terms.

Justifying a parent education program, for example, when clients must acquire new child care skills to learn age-appropriate expectations for a child is not difficult. Justification for requiring that clients attend counseling when an objective states that the client "must learn to recognize and respond to her child's need for affection" is difficult because the objective is vague. People are apt to disagree as to what constitutes a child's need for affection and outcome criteria would be largely subjective.

(3) *Services should be provided in the least restrictive setting.* In recent years, courts have ordered that services be provided in the least restrictive environment [6:193–268]. The implications for selecting service strategies are that services to maintain a child in her own home—emergency caretakers, homemakers, and day care, for example—are preferable to foster home placement unless there is clear evidence that the child cannot be safeguarded in her own home or that she has special treatment needs that cannot be met in the community.

(4) *Services must be feasible for a client.* Questions of feasibility are: "Does the client have the skills necessary to participate in a treatment program?" "Does the client have access to child care services at those times that she must go to parent education classes?" "Is transportation available and is there any conflict between the client's work schedule and the schedule of counseling or training sessions?"

(5) *Services should, when possible, be acceptable to the client.* As noted above, the client should participate in the selection of service strategies. Available alternatives, what each will require the client to do, and the changes that the client can expect from involvement should be described.

In reality, client choice may be limited. First, there may not be alternative methods of problem solving. Second, when clients are involuntary they may have no choice but to comply with service requirements deemed necessary to safeguard their children if they wish to retain or regain care of their youngsters.

(6) *Information describing previous services used by the client should be considered in selection of strategies.* Information descriptive of a client's previous use of services can be instructive for selection of treatment strategies if the methods employed and the outcomes attained were carefully documented. Thus, whether clients benefited from counseling, using any one or a mix of the methods described above, can inform workers as to the chances of success if similar methods are used for similar problems. Second, a client's knowledge of herself or her children—how they learn best—may

permit an evaluation of which approach or approaches are most likely to prove effective. Thus, the selection process may be facilitated if the methods used by counseling resources are described to clients and their input is encouraged.

WRITTEN SERVICE AGREEMENTS

Service Agreement—The Richards Family

The written service agreement developed for the Richards family is shown in figure 3.2. This initial agreement provided a framework for assessment. It was later amended to include problem-solving objectives, including a description of service strategies.

The results of Mr. Krasky's analysis of the taped conversations confirmed his hypothesis that mother and son were not able to discuss in a positive manner such sensitive issues as Larry's schooling, his household responsibilities, and his mother's expectations regarding the information that her son should share with her. Mrs. Richards, for example, gave Larry incomplete instructions, saying, "Come home early," without stating what "early" meant. Her perception (reported on the checklist she completed following the taped conversations) was that Larry should know what she meant. Larry's communications were delivered in a negative way, suggesting that his mother did not care what his opinion was.

The suggestion that Mrs. Richards's expectations were not realistic was confirmed in conversations with the worker. She did not, for instance, think that Larry should have any say in matters such as curfew time and household responsibilities. Moreover, when asked whether she thought that a young person of Larry's age had any right to privacy, she said no. "As long as he lives under my roof," she said, "he has to tell me where he is going, who he's with, and what he is doing."

Figure 3.2 **SERVICE AGREEMENT WITH THE RICHARDS FAMILY**

This agreement is entered into between Mrs. Amelia Richards, her son Larry Richards, who is currently residing in his mother's home, and Mr. Thomas Krasky, Child Welfare Worker for the Unified County Department of Social Services.

GOAL   To maintain Larry Richards in his own home.
OBJECTIVE   To complete problem assessment.
TASKS

Larry and Amelia Richards agree to:

1. Meet with Mr. Krasky once each week for 3 consecutive weeks beginning October 10, 1981. Each meeting will last approximately 2 hours from 4 P.M. to 6 P.M. and will take place in Mr. Krasky's office.

2. Working independently, identify three topics of conversation important to them, the discussion of which is difficult for them.

3. Discuss these topics during meetings with Mr. Krasky. Furthermore, they agree to have the conversations taped by the worker.

4. Report their thoughts and feelings regarding the conversations immediately following each of the discussions referred to in point 3, using a checklist prepared by Mr. Krasky.

5. Meet individually with Mr. Krasky during the second hour of each meeting. This time will be used to clarify issues that arise during the conversations and to discuss any general topics of concern to either client. Larry agrees to discuss issues related to his schooling.

6. Larry agrees to attend school for 10 consecutive days, beginning Monday, October 7, 1981.

Mr. Krasky agrees to:

1. Analyze the contents of the tapes and client self-reports within 5 working days of each session.

2. Share the results of this analysis with both members of the family, highlighting the strengths and weaknesses identified.

3. Develop a program to resolve identified difficulties or to identify a professional person in the community with the expertise to assist the Richards in problem resolution.

4. Explain to the Richards family the method chosen to resolve difficulties.

TIME LIMITS   The tasks listed above are to be completed within 30 days from the date of this agreement.

This agreement will be amended to describe the changes in family life that constitute problem resolution once assessment is complete. The procedures to be followed to resolve problems, including the responsibilities of both clients, Mr. Krasky, and a resource person, if used, will be described. If there are alternative ways of resolving identified difficulties, each will be described to the clients, whose input in selecting a problem-solving method will be encouraged.

CONSEQUENCES   Mr. Krasky agrees to discontinue this case in the child welfare agency contingent upon attaining the objectives that will be reported in the amended agreement. Failure to achieve objectives will result in a report to Larry's school indicating that the worker is not able to assist the family.

Moreover, the Richards understand that continued truancies by Larry could result in a report to the County Juvenile Court.

SIGNATURES

_____   _____
James Krasky, Child Welfare Worker   Amelia Richards

_____   _____
Larry Richards   Date

Amending Service Agreements

Initial service agreements may require modification. This can occur for different reasons. As with the Richards family, the first agreement may be written to provide a framework for assessment. Here, the fact that the document will be amended to report objectives and to describe procedures for achieving objectives is known at the outset, as is clear from the statement, "This agreement will be amended." A further reason for modifying agreements lies in recognizing that assessment is a continuing process. Problems not identified during the early stages of assessment may be observed at a later time. Or data gathered while monitoring client progress in achieving objectives may not show changes in problematic behaviors, causing the worker to reconsider his initial hypotheses regarding controlling conditions and to alter the approach to problem solving. Or parents or children may become ill, forcing cancellation of visits and necessitating an extension of the time limits established for visiting. Hypothetically, then, any agreement is subject to modification.

When agreements are first formulated, they should include a clause stating that it is possible that changes will be made. The statement, "This agreement is subject to change if additional problems are identified that would create risk for a child if not resolved," is illustrative. By noting that amendments will be made only if problems creating risk for children are identified, clients have a measure of protection against arbitrary demands for change. By including this clause in the initial agreement and by discussing some of the conditions that might necessitate changes in the plan, clients are prepared for possible revisions. Absent such preparation, even if the conditions for amending the document are reasonable, the client may perceive changes as arbitrary and the worker as creating obstacles to achievement of goals and objectives.

The amendment for Larry and Mrs. Richards is shown in figure 3.3. When amendments are written, each item that is changed on the initial agreement is marked with an asterisk, and a corresponding asterisk is marked on the amendment.

Mrs. Richards was required to attend a parents group at a local community mental health center to help her acquire knowledge of age-appropriate behaviors. The group was made up of parents of teen-agers, all of whom had difficulties similar to those that this client was experiencing.

Through a group discussion format, the leader sought to help parents understand some of the ways that teen-agers try to establish independence and to develop an appreciation for the fact that such efforts are a normal part of a youngster's development. The leader reviewed issues likely to cause difficulties between parents and their children, such as a young person's wish for privacy, which might cause a teen-ager to withhold information from a parent, and the importance to a teen-ager of peer approval, which could

Figure 3.3 **AMENDMENT TO SERVICE AGREEMENT WITH THE RICHARDS FAMILY**

*OBJECTIVES**

1. Amelia and Larry Richards will demonstrate skills for discussion of problematic issues and the skills necessary to negotiate problem resolution in a positive manner. (See fig. 3.4.)

2. Mrs. Richards will demonstrate knowledge of age-appropriate behavior for a youngster of Larry's age. (See below.)

3. Larry Richards will continue to attend school every day, except when excused for illness, for the period of this agreement.

*TIME LIMITS***

Extended for a period of 90 days, from November 27, 1981 to February 28, 1982.

SIGNATURES

_____   _____
James Krasky, Child Welfare Worker   Amelia Richards

_____   _____
Larry Richards   Date

---

result in behaviors distasteful to the parent. The strength of peer approval in maintaining behavior and the limits parents confronted in countering the influence of peers were considered.

Mrs. Richards agreed to attend and participate in group discussions and she gave her permission for the group leader to share information with Mr. Krasky describing her progress in the group.

The service agreement with the Innes family is shown in figure 3.5. Figures 3.6 through 3.8 describe the plans for meeting the problem-solving objectives reported in the service agreement.

Service Agreement—The Innes Family

Mr. Innes recorded assessment information in an uneven manner. For example, he made an average of only four recordings each day. Of these, a total of three corresponded in time and substance to the nine arguments reported by Mrs. Innes over the 12-day recording period. Thirty-four of the remaining 45 recordings he made (75%) were negative. In almost all instances he was alone when he recorded his mood. His commentary reflected

Figure 3.4   PLAN FOR NEGOTIATION TRAINING*

The objective of this program is to teach Larry and Amelia Richards methods of discussing issues about which there are differences of opinion, so that these differences can be resolved in a manner that is satisfactory to both parties. To accomplish this, Mr. Krasky agrees to do the following:

1. To meet with mother and son each Thursday evening between the hours of 5:30 and 7 P.M. The focus of these meetings will be as follows:
   a. To teach each party how to express an issue of concern in a specific manner so that the other person understands the focus of the concern.
   b. To facilitate step a, the worker will teach mother and son how to paraphrase what the other has said. Paraphrasing involves having the listener repeat, in his or her own words, what he or she has heard the speaker say. The speaker responds by stating either agreement or disagreement with what has been said.
   c. Finally, the worker will assist mother and son in learning how to "trade" to resolve differences of opinion. Trading involves identifying what each party is willing to give or contribute to problem resolution.

Mother and son agree to:

1. Be at home during each regularly scheduled meeting.
2. Practice the tasks learned during negotiation session. These practice sessions will occur on _____ in _____ and at no other time.
                                   (time)   (place)
3. In any practice area in which there is disagreement or difficulty, both parties agree to write down their view of the difficulty. This should include a statement of the aspect of negotiation training (e.g., being specific, paraphrasing, trading) that is difficult. Within the identified area of difficulty, each party should write down who was speaking, what was said, and their perception of the difficulty and how it could have been resolved.
4. The worker agrees to go over any issues that are listed and to assist mother and son in methods of resolving them.

*This plan was modeled after one described by Stein and Gambrill [7:114].

Figure 3.5   SERVICE AGREEMENT WITH THE INNES FAMILY

This agreement is entered into between Norma and James Innes, their children Michael and Linda, age 15 and 8 respectively, and Janice Cook, Child Welfare Worker for the County Department of Social Services.

GOAL   To maintain the Innes family intact.

OBJECTIVE 1   To divide household responsibilities among family members and to maintain the schedule established for the completion of household chores. (See attached.)

OBJECTIVE 2   To increase and maintain the frequency with which Mr. Innes engages in activities he identifies as positive. (See attached.)

OBJECTIVE 3   To establish a men's group, which Mr. Innes agrees to attend on a regular basis. (See attached.)

CONSEQUENCES   Ms. Cook agrees to discontinue protective service contingent upon family compliance with the plans established to attain the three goals reported above. Failure to comply with this agreement will require continued protective service supervision and may result in a report to the juvenile court.

TIME LIMITS   This agreement will be in effect for ninety (90) days from _____, to _____.

SIGNED

_____   _____
Norma Innes   James Innes

_____   _____
Michael Innes   Linda Innes

_____
Janice Cook, Child Welfare Worker

Figure 3.6   **PLAN TO MAINTAIN A DIVISION OF RESPONSIBILITY FOR HOUSEHOLD CHORES**

	M	TU	W	TH	F	SAT	SUN

Norma Innes

Prepare breakfast 4 days each week
Prepare menus for the week
Compile shopping list
Iron clothes
Prepare dinner 4 nights each week
Wash laundry on weekends

James Innes
   Prepare breakfast 3 days each week
   Clean up after breakfast on weekdays
   Grocery shopping
   Prepare dinner 3 nights each week

Michael Innes
   Clean up after breakfast 1 day each
      weekend
   Clean up after dinner
      Wash dishes
      Empty trash
      Put dishes away
   Vacuum on weekends

Linda Innes
   Clean up after breakfast 1 day each
      weekend
   Clean up after dinner
      clear table
      dry dishes
      sweep floor
   Fold laundry
   Dust on weekends

Instructions
      Each time that a chore is completed, place a check next to the name of the
person completing the task in the column showing the day of the week.
      Cleaning up after dinner is to be completed within one hour of the end of
mealtime.
      If problems are encountered in complying with this plan, family members
will not try to resolve difficulties on their own. Rather, they agree to contact
Ms. Cook as soon as possible after the problem arises. Ms. Cook agrees to meet
with family members at the earliest possible time to assist them with problem
solving.
      Ms. Cook will telephone the Innes home every other day for 10 days to
monitor compliance with this plan. She will review the chore completion
checklist at biweekly meetings with the family.

Figure 3.7 PLAN TO INCREASE THE FREQUENCY WITH WHICH MR. INNES ENGAGES IN ACTIVITIES THAT HE IDENTIFIES AS POSITIVE

Mr. Innes agrees to:
   1. Create a list of activities that he finds rewarding;
   2. Select one or two activities from the list that he can undertake immedi-
      ately;

3. Spend a minimum of 1½ hours each day engaging in an identified activity or activities;
4. Establish a daily schedule that indicates the time that he will spend in the identified activities that also allows time to complete household chores.

Ms. Cook agrees to:
1. Identify a range of volunteer activities that Mr. Innes can engage in;
2. Review the list with Mr. Innes and help him select an activity or activities that he thinks he would like to undertake;
3. Arrange for Mr. Innes to meet with the person or persons responsible for organizing the volunteer activity;
4. Meet with Mr. Innes once every other week and maintain telephone contact on alternate weeks to discuss his thoughts and feelings regarding his use of time.

Figure 3.8 **PLAN TO ESTABLISH A MEN'S GROUP**

Ms. Cook agrees to:
1. Meet with Mr. Carleton, Director of Northside Community Mental Health, to identify a counselor who is willing to establish a men's group;
2. Assist in whatever way possible in identifying others to participate in the group;
3. Monitor Mr. Innes's attendance at the group meetings and meet with the client and group leader to discuss any difficulties that arise in regard to Mr. Innes's participation and attendance.

Mr. Innes agrees to:
1. Meet with the group leader and to identify others who might be interested in participating in the group;
2. Attend and participate in group meetings on a regular basis;
3. Meet with Ms. Cook and the group leader should the need arise. (See item 3: Ms. Cook's tasks.)

---

boredom (noting, for example, that "I have nothing to do except hang around the house"), and pessimism about finding work ("Nothing in today's want ads—no sense in applying for jobs, there aren't any around"). As before, his positive moods were related to talking with friends who were also unemployed.

The majority of disputes between husband and wife were in relation to her work (seven of the nine), with a substantive focus on Mr. Innes's unwillingness to assume responsibility for household management. In only two of the quarrels was the subject of money mentioned.

There was little discrepancy between the records of father and son. Ten of the 12 recording days were school days. Michael had come directly home on 9 of these days, had done his chores without discussion, and, with a single exception, in a satisfactory manner.

This information was not congruent with what was reported by Mr. Innes during early meetings with Ms. Cook, although it supported Michael's view of his own behavior. One could offer a variety of hypotheses to explain the discrepancy. The father's initial report could have been unduly biased, given his extreme pessimism. Or, father and son could have deliberately misrepresented information in this area since a negative report would draw attention to their interaction as causal to Michael's injuries. But Mr. Innes's earlier report could have been correct and Michael's behavior subsequently modified by the fight with his father, by the fact of protective service intervention, or by the act of self-monitoring. Ms. Cook shared her analysis of the data with the family and noted the conflict in the information reported by father and son. Mr. Innes said that Michael had changed and was doing a good job with his chores.

Three areas of difficulty are highlighted in the assessment data: household management, and Mr. Innes's boredom and his pessimism about work. With regard to the first issue, Ms. Cook suggested that family members list all chores that had to be done, including the frequency with which chores had to be completed. She suggested that they work together to divide responsibility for identified tasks in a manner that was acceptable to all family members.

Speaking to Mr. Innes, Ms. Cook suggested two ways of dealing with his difficulties. As to his boredom, she asked that he give some thought to activities, hobbies, for example, that he might undertake on a regular basis. And she inquired into whether he would consider doing some volunteer work in the community in his spare time. If so, she would be responsible for identifying alternatives from which he could select one or two that had appeal. Then she asked if he would be willing to become part of a men's group comprised of others who were unemployed. Ms. Cook pointed out that Mr. Innes's records showed that his good feelings fluctuated in relation to information that he received from others whose situation was similar to his own, where similarities seemed to add balance to his perspective of his circumstances. "I think that you are blaming yourself for a situation over which you have no control," Ms. Cook said. She concluded by noting that if Mr. Innes would consider joining such a group, she would take responsibility for contacting someone to start one.

MONITORING CLIENT PROGRESS
IN SERVICE DELIVERY PROGRAMS

The worker who is responsible for implementing the case plan must monitor client progress in attaining the goals and objectives of the plan. Implementation and monitoring are generally not intake functions; rather, they are the responsibility of the service worker. However, they are of sufficient importance to merit a brief discussion [7:65–97].

In general, the procedures used to gather assessment data are sufficient for continual monitoring. For example, Mr. Innes can be asked to continue to monitor his moods, using the form on which he reported assessment data. If engaging in personal activities and in the men's group have the intended effect, this should be reflected by an increase in the frequency with which the client records positive feelings, and a decrease in negative feelings. Changes in mood should be associated with undertaking new activities and group participation.

Likewise, continued taping of conversations between Larry and Mrs. Richards and subsequent analysis of tapes should yield evidence of acquisition of new communication skills. If skill acquisition and modification of Mrs. Richards's expectations have the desired effect of reducing problems at home and at school, this would be evidenced by client self-reports and in Larry's grade reports and school attendance records.

If, however, there is no change, or if there is improvement at home but not at school, the worker will have to reassess the situation (here, identifying ways of gathering data regarding Larry's larger social environment assumes relevance) and develop new service strategies.

Information gathered while monitoring client compliance with case plans becomes the basis for deciding to amend the plan to give the client a further opportunity to realize goals, or if appropriate, to terminate the case in the child welfare agency, or to pursue alternative permanent plans for the children [4;5;2;7].

FOR DISCUSSION

Using the case that you selected for task number 2, chapter 2, do the following:

TASK ONE

Identify the appropriate case goal.

TASK TWO

Write one case objective for each problem for which services will be provided.
Write out the tasks that client(s) and the worker must undertake to achieve the objectives.
Describe feasible problem-solving strategies for attaining each objective and provide a rationale for their selection.

TASK THREE

Write a service plan that includes:

1. the names of the parties involved
2. the case goal
3. problem-solving objectives
4. tasks
5. problem-solving strategies
6. time limits
7. consequences

REFERENCES

1. Eileen D. Gambrill, and Kermit T. Wiltse. "Foster Care: Plans and Actualities." *Public Welfare* 32 (Spring, 1974).
2. Eileen D. Gambrill, and Theodore J. Stein. *Supervision in Child Welfare: A Training Manual.* Berkeley, CA: University of California Extension Press, 1978.
3. Shirley Jenkins, and Mignon Sauber. *Paths to Child Placement.* New York: Columbia University Press, 1966.
4. Martha L. Jones, and John L. Biesecker. *Permanency Planning Guide for Children and Youth Services.* Millersville, PA: Millersville State College, Training Resources in Permanent Planning Project, n.d.
5. Victor Pike et al. *Permanent Planning for Children in Foster Care: A Handbook for Social Workers.* Portland, OR: Regional Research Institute for Human Services, Portland State University, 1977.
6. Richard Rapson. "The Right of the Mentally Ill to Receive Treatment in the Community." *Columbia Journal of Law and Social Problems* 16 (1980).
7. Theodore J. Stein, and Eileen D. Gambrill. *Decision Making in Foster Care: A Training Manual.* Berkeley, CA: University of California Extension Press, 1976.
8. Theodore J. Stein. "An Overview of Services to Families and Children to Prevent Placement and to Facilitate Family Reunification." In Mark Hardin, ed., *Foster Children in the Courts.* Woburn, MA: Butterworth, in press.
9. United States Senate, Committee on Finance. *Adoption Assistance and Child Welfare Act of 1980.* 96th Congress, 2nd session. Washington, D.C.: U.S. Government Printing Office, June 17, 1980, pp. 500–535. States must comply with the provisions of the Act in order to receive federal funding.
10. Dennis R. Young, and Richard R. Nelson. *Public Policy for Day Care of Young Children: Organization, Finance and Planning.* Lexington, MA: D.C. Heath and Co., 1973.